Great for individuals or small study groups, this guide will help you get the most out of *Friendship in the Lord*.

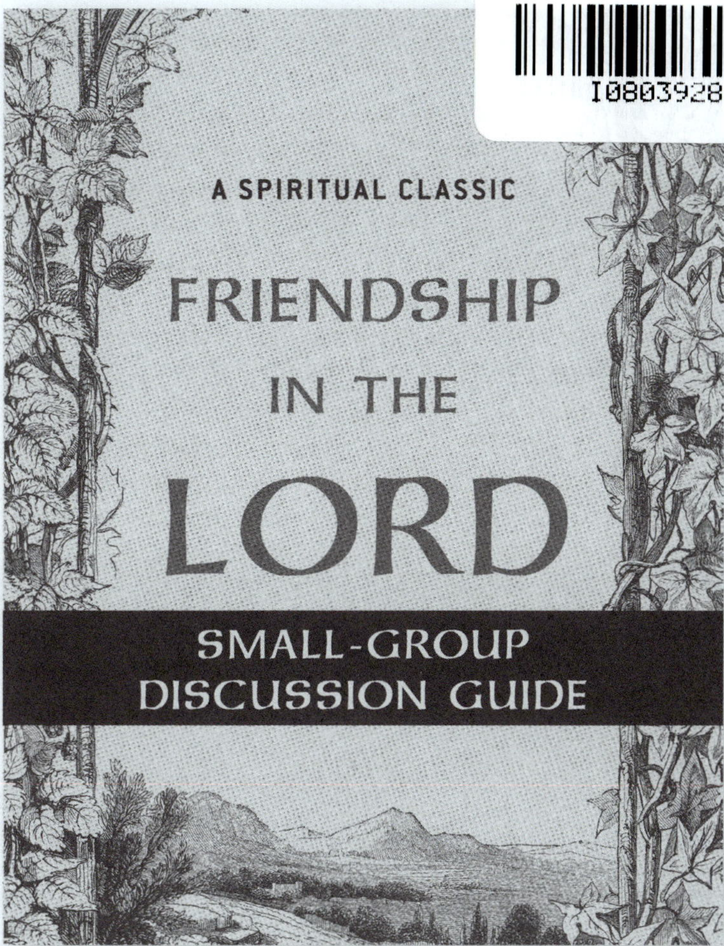

Scan here to download the complete printable guide or visit **avemariapress.com/products/friendship-in-the-lord-small-group-guide**.

"I've never before finished a book so inspired to be a better husband, son, brother, friend, and disciple of Jesus. This book was truly transformational! 10/10 recommend. 100/100. 1,000/1,000!"

Tanner Kalina

Cofounder of the *Saints Alive* podcast and author of *Aching for Greatness*

"G. K. Chesterton once observed that our 'root horror' in this human ordeal is isolation. Especially as we undergo this 'epidemic of loneliness,' we need friendship if we are to flourish. Our friendships help us to enter into life and into relationship with the Lord, who reveals himself as our most beloved Friend. In this book, Fr. Hinnebusch gives a beautifully balanced account of friendship, at once sensibly sensitive to its emotional and psychological complexity and keenly aware of its spiritual fruits. His work is a great gift to all of us on the way."

Fr. Gregory Pine, OP

Instructor of dogmatic and moral theology at the Dominican House of Studies and assistant director of the Thomistic Institute

"This book felt like a feast, satiating me with the best of truths. God is the God of love! He extends his loving friendship to all of us, and in turn, we have the privilege of entering into divine friendship with him and all of his children. What good news! This book is perfect for a small-group setting or for anyone who wants to grow in the spirituality of friendship."

Maggie Craig

Catholic speaker and author of *Friendship Reset*

"Fr. Hinnebusch shows with clarity and tenderness how true Christian friendship calls us to vulnerability, honesty, and trust. It can be challenging, but when rooted in the Lord, true friends can be vessels of grace who pour forth and draw out the very best in one another. *Friendship in the Lord* reminds us that the purpose of friendship is not just companionship but also sanctification."

Chika Anyanwu and Mari Pablo

Catholic speakers (and friends in Christ)

"This is one of the most wonderfully helpful books I have ever read. Rare is the text that treats a topic of such universal importance and so easily reaches into the core of human yearning with the guiding light of theological truth. In a remarkably approachable and invitational manner, Fr. Paul Hinnebusch ushers us along a pathway proven by his own integrated experience, experience confirmed by and refined within the light of theology. Fr. Hinnebusch marks out this pathway by the humble offering of simple and tender insights that dispel fear and magnify the radiance of true friendship. This present edition comes at a time when its themes are as needed as ever."

From the foreword by Fr. John Burns
Priest of the Archdiocese of Milwaukee and
founder of Friends of the Bridegroom

"When I first read this book many years ago, it forever changed my view of friendship and how to honor and reverence the Lord, myself, and others. As I have pondered the many friendships in my own life over the years, I have seen both joy and sorrow, darkness and light. In rereading this work by Fr. Paul Hinnebusch, I was filled again with the desire to give to the Lord every relationship in my life and receive each one of them again through his heart."

From the afterword by Sr. Miriam James Heidland, SOLT
Popular author and speaker, cohost of the *Abiding Together* podcast,
and retreat leader for priests and religious sisters

FRIENDSHIP IN THE LORD

A SPIRITUAL CLASSIC

PAUL HINNEBUSCH, OP

Christian Classics *Notre Dame, Indiana*

Scripture translation by the author.

Nihil Obstat: Reverend Monsignor Michael Heintz, PhD
Censor librorum
Imprimatur: Most Reverend Kevin C. Rhoades
Bishop of Fort Wayne–South Bend
Given at Fort Wayne, Indiana, on August 20, 2025

First published in book form under the title *Friendship in the Lord*, Ave Maria Press, 1974.

Founded in 1865, Ave Maria Press is a ministry of the United States Province of Holy Cross.

www.avemariapress.com/christian-classics

Paperback: ISBN-13 978-0-87061-328-9

E-book: ISBN-13 978-0-87061-329-6

Cover images © Getty Images.

Cover and text design by Brianna Dombo Nicholson.

Printed and bound in the United States of America.

TO ALL MY FRIENDS
WHO HAVE TAUGHT ME HOW
TO REJOICE IN LOVE.

CONTENTS

FOREWORD

BY FR. JOHN BURNS

The book you hold in your hands is one of the most wonderfully helpful books I have ever read. Rare is the text that treats a topic of such universal importance and so easily reaches into the core of human yearning with the guiding light of theological truth.

We know it to be the case both by intuition and experience: Life simply cannot be lived to its full in the absence of communion and community. We have a word for the relationship of love that exists between two or more people who strive for rightly ordered communion: We call them *friends*. Jesus used this word to explain how we are best to understand our relationship with him: "No longer do I call you servants . . .; but I have called you friends" (Jn 15:15).

Every single one of us longs for meaningful, lasting, loyal relationships. We are made for friendship—we thrive in it; it delights us. For good reason, friendship has been a frequent topic of both casual and scholarly consideration for all of history. Among the many brilliant works that make up the marvelous backdrop of the book you are about to enjoy, we cannot overlook the timelessness of Aristotle's treatment of friendship in the *Nicomachean Ethics* or the richness of St. Aelred of Rievaulx's *Spiritual Friendship*. In more recent times, St. John Paul II's short essay *A Meditation on Givenness* might be the most compact and illuminative summary to date.

Friendship in the Lord adds something of great worth to the category of writings in which it resides. In a remarkably approachable and invitational manner, Fr. Paul Hinnebusch ushers us along a pathway proven by his own integrated experience, experience confirmed by and refined within the light of theology. Fr. Hinnebusch marks out this pathway by the humble offering of simple and tender insights that dispel fear and magnify the radiance of true friendship. This present edition, a republication of the out-of-print original, comes at a time when its themes are as needed as ever.

A NEW EDITION

The story of the publication of this new edition goes back to my early days of seminary. One afternoon during my first few weeks in Rome, I was invited to assist at a little soup kitchen just down the hill from our house of studies. There, I encountered an absolutely delightful religious sister. She was full of joy—luminous, really. She masterfully modeled rightly ordered relationships with her sisters, with priests, with volunteers, and with the poor in a manner that was so *attractive* that everyone just wanted to be near her, to learn from her, to help her, even just to sit within her radius.

I would quickly learn, to nobody's great surprise, that the deep font of her gracious joy was an intimate love of God. Yet the way that love flowed out of her and into the love of her neighbors—which theology calls the love of friendship—was something I had not quite seen before. It was the Gospel *lived*, and it generated an entire community of believers wholeheartedly engaging in the apostolate. I immediately sought to learn from her, and after several conversations on the topics of relationships, mission, and charity, she shared with me a tattered copy of a book by Fr. Paul Hinnebusch.

Admittedly, I was initially skeptical, both of the title and of its origin in the 1970s. But as I moved through it, I was captivated. I found answers to many questions I had not fully articulated, even to myself. I discovered insights into the themes of right order, priority, and gratuity within my existing network of relationships. I realized that some friendships had quite a bit of unrealized potential and that others may not be as sincere and deep as I had once thought. And I realized that I did not yet have in place the categories Fr. Hinnebusch provides for understanding friendship as so much more than a pleasant relationship from which both parties benefit. Rather, certain friendships are best understood as given by God, gifts that bring particular blessings as they also bring certain responsibilities.

I became convinced that this short text has so very much to offer in a time such as ours, and I am so delighted that it is now widely available. In order to help orient you to the contents of the book, and because no text on the topic of friendship is complete or perfect, this present volume warrants both a bit of precautionary framing and some hearty encouragement.

ON PRUDENCE AND FEAR

As experience demonstrates, friendship is not always a simple business. Friendship entails opening our lives to others, a process that raises a great many questions. Even if we can admit our profound longing for meaningful relationships, the matter of how to understand and engage true friendship can be a daunting one. As fine as the idea of true friendship can sound in theory, the choice to truly move into emotional intimacy, mutual trust, and appropriate vulnerability can provoke certain hesitations and even fears.

At the outset, let us recall that not all fear is problematic. The fear of sin is a well-ordered fear; we need it. I daresay, in introducing the topic of this book, that a healthy sense of sin and a humble recognition of one's own susceptibility to it are the prudential guardrails that prevent any misinterpretation or misapplication of the contents of the pages that follow.

Yet we must always sift the movements of our hearts to carefully distinguish between fear and prudence. Prudence instructs, teaches, guides, and informs. Fear gives rise to flight. When it is a disproportionate fear, it causes us to flee from good things, to close up and hide, to stop trying. Fear can cause us to lose the spirit of adventure that so classically characterizes the great human quest, our pilgrimage home. Prudence dictates thoughtful, careful entrance into every endeavor; it informs healthy boundaries. Fear, which often dresses up as prudence, actually encloses and even enslaves.

If we notice fear rising in our hearts around the topic of friendship, we might invite the Holy Spirit to enlighten us as to what is happening within. As we do, we typically discover layers of concern about our own stories, our history of relationships or perhaps the lack of them. We might notice fears about the proclivities of the heart, with all its power for good and also ill. Perhaps we discover a fear of finding ourselves in an agonizing echo of some past trauma. Maybe we notice the fear of becoming confused or confusing someone else. Faced with these many movements within, it sometimes seems safer to avoid the matter of real, intimate friendship altogether. In what might seem to be prudence, we deem it safer to just not engage, and we settle for seemingly easier means by which to meet our desire for intimacy.

Unfortunately, today we find many an opportunity to avoid confronting these inner movements altogether. Technology, so helpful in many ways, can often serve as an unhelpful crutch. In an age of screen-mediated interactivity, vast networks of digital "community" offer an apparent shortcut to the fulfillment of our desire for meaningful connection. These networks fool us into believing that our lives are marked by an abundance of friendship, when most of these relationships are largely insubstantial and require quite little of us. In a world of so many connections from the safety of our couches, our fundamental ache to really know and be known is superficially pacified by a host of quick and ready remedies that subtly bypass our actual needs.

Deep within, as we walk through an average day, we know that something is adrift in our culture, and something within us is quietly atrophied. We are at risk of forgetting our great capacity for relationship and our ability to grow, to mature, and to become better through communion with one another. Left unexamined, this atrophy agitates us until it fuels our coping mechanisms. In our efforts to satisfy the ache for the other, we turn to sin, disintegration, hiding, blame, and shame. Over time, callouses compound, and we lose the tender willingness to open and to be reverent, to cry out for help, to welcome others into our weakness and to bless others in theirs.

It is in these places that our Lord comes constantly to seek us out. And, from time to sacred time, God sends us friends to do the same.

FROM THE BEGINNING

From the beginning, it was friendship that rescued the first man. God saw that it was not good for Adam to be alone, and so God crafted another creature like in kind but distinct. When we look closely at the text of Genesis, we see that both the man and the woman began alone with God, and then God drew them together. For both, the discovery of the other brought a blossoming of heart, a realization that they had more to give and receive than they could have understood in their aloneness. This maturation marks the possibility of every human friendship, especially when friendship is held up to the light of grace.

When sin entered into creation's fabric, so, too, did the tendency to close up, to hide in rupture, and to turn away from God and one another. The friendship that marked humanity's origin quickly gave way to the weight of confusion, competition, rejection, and isolation.

Because the enemy labors with all his evil might against the works of God, one of sin's darkest whisperings is the lie that we must live alone, and we are better off if we do so. Does it not make sense, then, that the enemy would turn his resources against the good gift of friendship in every way conceivable?

And because the enemy will concede partial goods if they keep us from the greater good, we ought not be surprised to find a plethora of opportunities for relationships that are not true to their divine purpose.

MATURITY AND GROWTH

If we give in to the whispers of fear and choose to live alone, we can spend our whole lives never confronting our limits and imperfections. We may find it alluring to take that easier way, but that way is indeed but a temptation. If we succumb to it, the maturity of our hearts will remain woefully stunted.

When I begin to call someone a friend, I implicitly state something quite significant. Deep down, I admit that I *cannot* live alone, and I no longer wish to try. Once I admit that, I can begin to open myself and engage with an utterly unique and unrepeatable other, electing to discover and reverence a whole life with all of the glorious and messy details that make the friend particularly lovable. In the same movement, I welcome this friend to behold and discover who I truly am; I slowly come out of hiding and take the risk of allowing myself to be seen and cherished.

The dynamics of friendship are deeply etched with the contours of mutual discovery. What attracts us at first—the longing to see and be seen, to love and be loved—eventually brings us to make a choice to leave behind small, self-centered living. As we begin to trust others with the details of our stories, we gradually brush up against our limits. Because friendship is mutual, we also discover the limits of our friends. In friendship, rough edges cannot remain hidden, insecurities jostle to the surface, and the confines of our immaturity come into the light. Real friendship necessarily breaks down the false facade we present to the world; it draws us to recognize weakness and poverty, both in ourselves and in the beloved.

What differentiates true friendships from superficial ones is charity. When we find ourselves loved where we are broken, and when we love a friend in his or her poverty, the logic of grace is set in motion. A true friend is a sort of icon of God, an *other* through whom the Lord's kindness and mercy shine in a manner that binds up and anoints our brokenness.

It is right there, as we find ourselves not condemned but cherished, that we make the thrilling discovery of unrealized potential and the possibility of becoming *better*. As we choose to grow, we begin to see that we could never have truly unearthed our own poverty without the love of friendship. For in friendship, not only are we invited to grow, but we place ourselves at the service of the growth of the other. Together, we experience the rerouting of our expectations, happily surprised to be loved where we anticipated rejection. Fr. Hinnebusch puts it so well: "Intimacy is a love which accepts me fully even when it sees that I am far from perfect. It is a love which patiently nurtures in me whatever is imperfect, a love which always sees my potentialities for good and draws them to full blossom by the sun of appreciation" (24).

Pause for a moment, if you would, and imagine a world woven with networks of this kind of relationship. Imagine what it would do to cast out fear, to dispel the loneliness that leads to heartbreaking sin. Consider the violence and poverty we see in our world, and that the Gospel call to love our neighbor is deeply personal and quite practical. Consider what friendship could do to facilitate honest, authentic living as our "truest selves," to use a phrase Fr. Hinnebusch uses often.

It would be nearly impossible to exaggerate the importance of friendship or to overestimate it. Friendship has the power to heal our world; it is a means of communion, a participation in the very life of the Holy Trinity. Friendship, along with the cultivation of the habits and practices that sustain it, sits at the center of the question of where our world and our culture go from here.

SOME PRACTICAL COUNSELS

The republication of this book is important for all of these reasons. The insights and perspectives Fr. Hinnebusch offers throughout the pages that follow are very much at the service of a rediscovery of the great potential of true friendship.

A few considerations might help to frame how you engage not only the contents of the book but its implications. As you will discover, this is by no means a field guide to friendship, nor is it a manual of instruction on navigating the granular details of complex relationships. In fact, it does not contain as much practical instruction as one might expect. Rather, this book explores the nature of friendship when understood as a relationship given by and drawn up into the Lord. It outlines the principles essential to the highest form of friendship. And it invites us to step through our hesitations into a gift from God.

The beautiful themes of *Friendship in the Lord* will almost certainly open up many a rich conversation and a whole landscape of invitational possibilities. Because Fr. Hinnebusch treats the ordering principles of friendship in the Lord with less attention to practical questions, a real entrance into the themes of the book will require a stable life of prayer and willingness to engage mature, ongoing discernment. A word on both will hopefully assist the fruitful engagement of the book's contents.

First, a word on faith as the premise. All friendship, regardless of one's state in life, is best understood in relation to God. The Lord's actions and interventions in our lives are all in view of raising us up into greater goodness and more excellent pursuit of the final goal of human existence. As such, eyes of faith recognize the hand of God guiding the intersections of life's circumstances, including the invitation to share the journey with others as our friends.

We must attend to a distinction. On one hand, we desire authentic friendship with fervor; the ideas encapsulated in the pages ahead will cause your heart to swell. The longing for this kind of friendship is a good and holy one. Yet the presence of the desire does not suggest that every relationship we engage has the qualities and the potential so eloquently outlined in the pages to come.

When we speak of friendship as friendship *in the Lord*, we recall always that the Lord is first in everything; nothing whatsoever in friendship can ever displace that priority, the primacy of God. As Fr. Hinnebusch says so well, "What a Christian friend wants above all else for the loved one is his or her communion with the Lord. The one I love, my wife, my husband, my friend, belongs first of all to the Lord. And in that sense, I am only the friend of the Bridegroom. He alone is true Spouse of each and every human heart. He must increase, while I must decrease" (3). Indeed, friendship that comes from God always leads back to God. It is a gift, one we must receive with open hands and hearts.

We do not acquire gifts by our own power, nor can we fabricate this kind of friendship by sheer human effort. There is a great difference between seeking out friendship on our own and learning what it means to perceive God's movements inviting us into friendship. On the basis of this distinction, the practical key is simple: Rather than anxiously searching for relationships to save us from loneliness, we rest our hearts on the belief that God wants us to flourish. In a posture of surrender inclined first toward God, we ask in prayer for the gift of real friendship. This is the starting point of communion; when it is securely in place, it will save us from much confusion, squandered energy, and the snares of self-provision.

The second word of counsel follows upon the first. Once we recognize a friendship as a gift, we then welcome God to lead us along the way of discernment and growth. Absent good, principled discernment, an overzealous attempt to apply the themes of this book can easily lead to a loss of reverence around the boundaries of the heart. What may begin with good intentions can quickly degenerate into disregard for right order. Because this type of friendship is given by God, it grows in the light; it flowers as we behold shared questions, struggles, joys, and delights *with God*. Because it is God who draws every true set of friends together, it is also God who speaks order, with both affirmation and correction, into the hearts of the friends who, at best, listen both individually and together for God's voice.

In light of these two matters, the best of friendships are marked by faith, humility, and a willingness to learn and grow. Without mutual faith, friendship will always have a substantial limit. In faith, the limits of friendship are set by God, who mysteriously draws us more and more deeply into charity. And charity has no upper limit.

This, in essence, is the Christian life. It is what I first saw in that constellation of community that swirled around the sisters and their apostolate in Rome. I have so happily learned that the good things I observed there were by no means limited to those circumstances and settings. Rather, those were privileged moments of observing what it really looks like to follow Jesus, and what is possible when we open our lives in trust and welcome his gifts.

In the gospels, when he was asked about the greatest commandment, Jesus noted two: to love the Lord God above all else, and to love one's neighbor as oneself (see Matthew 22:37–39). You are about to enjoy a book brimming with inspirations and invitations that will most certainly assist you in both. I am filled with hope that it will bless you and those with whom you walk along the paths of friendship in the Lord.

PREFACE

This book is a friendship telling its story. It is friends telling together their experience of friendship in the Lord.

A friendship is two lives joined in love and lived as one. But friendship in the Lord is never two people closed in upon themselves. Each of the friends is fully open to the Lord and open to other friends in such a way that the friendship is always part of a larger community. The Christian community is a cluster of many friendships knit together.

This is the autobiography of such a cluster of friends. It is the fruit of reflection upon our experience of friendship.

This friendship was also an experience of life in the Holy Spirit, and therefore the book is really a combination of Christian witness and theological reflection.

We present this book in the form of witness rather than mere theological reflection, because we have learned from experience that the only theology which moves others is the theology which is rooted in genuine Christian experience and has been personally lived. Only living witness really moves others.

Also, from my own experience of lecturing to young religious and seminarians, I realized that I would have to talk about human friendship before I could talk about intimate friendship with the Persons of the Holy Trinity in prayer. Yet I knew that to speak of one independently of the other would be a distortion of the Christian reality. I would have to integrate the two elements into one book. It is difficult to speak of one without neglecting the other.

That is why the book seesaws back and forth between human friendship and divine friendship, hoping that the reader will ultimately get some grasp of how the two aspects must be completely integrated into our lives if we are to live fully the life of the Spirit. In other words, direct loving contemplation of God and loving service to others must coexist in a balanced blend in every Christian life.

Lastly, since celibacy for the sake of the Lord is a charismatic witness bearing a message for all Christians, we have endeavored to apply our insights to all our fellow Christians, and especially to married people and their way of living the one mystery of Christ, the only Bridegroom of his people.

I am convinced that this book has as much to say to married people as it does to priests and other consecrated celibates. It is addressed to all Christians who are seeking a contemporary Christian spirituality.

I wish to acknowledge my special indebtedness to Sr. Mary Ann Fatula, OP, head of the Department of Religion, Northwest Catholic High School, West Hartford, Connecticut. While this book was being written, she and I carried on a series of conversations on friendship. These were the continuation of an evening of reflection on friendship in which we had engaged with a circle of friends. The conversations were recorded on tape and later incorporated almost verbatim into the book.

At least forty pages of the book are Sr. Mary Ann's own words. Another twenty pages were directly inspired by her words as I responded to her either in the conversations or in later reflection upon what she had said. I express my sincere appreciation of her special contribution to this book.

Paul Hinnebusch, OP
Bishop Lynch Priory
Dallas, Texas

PROLOGUE

"I MUST DECREASE"

Once upon a time there was a loyal servant of a great lord. The lord's castle overlooked a stormy channel, separating his domain from the homeland of a lovely lady. The servant, in charge of the lord's archives, had come across an ancient parchment proving that the servant, not the lord, was the true and lawful heir to the domain.

The servant secretly loved the beautiful lady. He had come to know her when he accompanied the lord on visits to her. When he found the wonderful parchment, he decided that at an opportune moment he would not only claim his lawful heritage, but would also ask the lady's hand in marriage. For now he would be of her rank, and she would not disdain him.

One evening he heard that the lady was on her way across the channel to visit the lord. This would be his chance. On her arrival he would bring forth the document from the folds of his garments and claim both his heritage and his lady.

As the day drew near its close, the servant accompanied the lord down to the shores of the channel, and together they paced the sea wall, waiting for the arrival of the lady's boat. But a great storm came up, and the boat was caught in rain and adverse winds. A pitch-black darkness fell over sea and shore. Fearing that the boat would not find its way in the darkness, the lord ordered a fire to be lighted to serve as a beacon. But nothing would burn. The heavy rains had drenched every bit of combustible material. There was no dry tinder to catch a spark, no dry moss or shavings of wood to use in starting a blaze.

Fearing that the lady would drown in the storm, the servant pulled out the precious parchment, the only hope and proof of his future, and set it ablaze. The boatman saw the flame, steered a right course in the darkness, and brought the boat safely to dock.

The lady disembarked and flew to the arms of the lord in loving surrender. The servant listened to the lord's voice, welcoming the lady in tender words of ardent love. His heart, victorious over his own disappointment, rejoiced in the happiness of the lady he loved, and the happiness of the lord whom he loyally served and loved as a friend. The words of John the Baptist came to his mind: "The bridegroom's friend, who stands by and listens to him, is overjoyed at hearing the bridegroom's voice. This joy, this perfect joy, is now mine" (Jn 3:29).

In the depths of his heart the servant set up the coat of arms of his true nobility, inscribed with John's words: "He must increase, but I must decrease" (Jn 3:29).

This is the story of St. Joseph even before it is the story of John the Baptist. It is the story of every one of us. No true lover ever imprisons his loved one in his own possessiveness. He gives her distance, he even steps out of her life, if necessary, that she might become what God calls her to be.

The angel instructs Joseph concerning the divine mystery at work in Mary: "Joseph," he says, "God the Most High, through the power of his Spirit, has espoused Mary like a bride, and has fashioned her child in her womb. In reverence for your beloved Mary, let her be her noblest self! Let her have her deep relationship with the Lord God, and she will be all the more precious to you!"

The response to this in Joseph's heart must have been a joyful, "He must increase, but I must decrease." Joseph gives Mary her distance. He stands aside that she might become fully the person God meant her to be: spouse of the Holy Spirit and mother of a divine work of love, knitting all mankind together in love. And yet, in the wonders of God's love, Joseph nevertheless receives Mary as his own, and with her he receives God too! "Joseph, son of David, do not be afraid to take Mary home with you as your wife. It is by the Holy Spirit that she has conceived this child. She will bear a son; and you shall give him the name Jesus (Mt 1:20). As husband of his mother, you shall have the father's privilege of giving him his name. You shall have him as your son, for you shall have his mother as your wife."

To this, the response in Joseph's heart must have been a joyous, "Yes, I must decrease, but I need not disappear from her life!" Reverently letting Mary be her true self, Joseph's tender love for her was all the richer in receiving her. Willingly he accepted to live with her in celibacy. For in his loving reverence, he respected her as bride of the Lord God and accepted the fittingness that she remain forever a virgin. "Though I must decrease, yet I shall have the joy of continuing to love her and live in her love."

Since love desires that the beloved be his or her truest self, and one's truest self is found in communion with the Lord, all love must have the celibate spirit: profound reverence for the beloved as belonging to the Lord! Sooner or later everyone who loves must face the reality that the Lord has entered into the life of the one we love; and each friend will have to say, "He must increase, I must decrease."

For the Lord alone can satisfy the human heart. In every heart there are infinite depths which no human friend can fill, depths which only God can fill. Realizing this, Christian husband and wife appreciate what Paul means when he says that they will probably want to abstain at times from conjugal relations, by mutual consent, to give themselves to prayer (1 Cor 7:5).

What a Christian friend wants above all else for the loved one is his or her communion with the Lord. The one I love, my wife, my husband, my friend, belongs first of all to the Lord. And in that sense, I am only the friend of the Bridegroom. He alone is true Spouse of each and every human heart. He must increase, while I must decrease.

If I do not learn this lesson early in my love for another, I must certainly learn it when I myself am called to my Lord in death. To meet him and to be fully united with him in glory, I must separate from everyone else whom I love. When I die, I must leave my wife or husband, my children, my friends, my lands, my power and achievements, my very body. Only when I have left all else can I receive his total embrace, for which I was created.

To witness to this fact, that the Lord is the true Bridegroom of every human person, some people do not wait until death forces them to leave all things. In consecrated celibacy, they leave everything at the outset of their youthful lives so that their whole lives and all their energies may be a running to the Lord, the Bridegroom who alone can satisfy the human heart.

But just as Joseph, even while he decreased, received Mary again from God, to be loved tenderly and cherished as his wife, so too the celibate is given many persons to love and carries on a mission of universal love, mediating God's own love. Anyone who gives the Lord the central place in his love will be all the richer in his love of others. And everyone who, in death, departs from all else to be with the Lord will receive again, in the Lord, all those whom he has rightly loved.

If, in the great knitting together in covenant love (Col 2:2), we are woven into more profound intimacy with some than with others, it is always the Lord Jesus who is closest of all to each one of us, closer to each than his wife or her husband or other dear friend. If we can love one another with his own heart, it is only because he is the true Bridegroom of every heart.

PART ONE

ONE

THE MINISTRY OF FRIENDSHIP

I had been asked to speak about the spirituality of a deacon before a group of thirty-one candidates for the permanent diaconate for the Diocese of Dallas. Twenty-nine of these men were married. The occasion gave me an excellent opportunity for reflecting on the subject of friendship.

The word "deacon" means "servant." Yet Jesus says, "I call you servants no longer, I have called you friends." The address to the deacons, prepared at a time when I was filled with the glow of the joy of Christian friendship, was the fruit of reflection upon my experience of friendship as a true ministry or service in the Church.

I had been back home visiting my family and my friends. In each home I visited, we experienced a remarkable presence of God's own love and friendship expressed in our gatherings. I came back to my work greatly refreshed, determined to write a book on the joy of friendship as a sharing in the joy which the three divine Persons of the Holy Trinity find in communion with one another.

The mission of joy and friendship within the Christian community is even more fundamental than the Church's mission to the poor and needy, because love and joy are the source from which all ministry to the sorrowing must flow.

NOT SERVANTS BUT FRIENDS

"I call you servants no longer; a servant does not know what his master is about. I have called you friends, because I have made known to you all that I have heard from my Father" (Jn 15:13–15).

Although these words were addressed first of all to the apostles at the Last Supper, they were meant for everyone who believes in Jesus. To each one he says, "I call you servants no longer; I have called you friends."

In saying this, Jesus does not deny that we are his servants, and he does not deny that he is Lord. Rather, he brings out the true nature of his lordship and shows the true nature of our service. We are servants of his love, we are ministers of his friendship, we carry on his own mission of love and friendship. We can do this only if we are truly his friends.

The Lord was sent by his Father on a mission of love. "As the Father has loved me, so I have loved you. Dwell in my love. . . . There is no greater love than this, that a man should lay down his life for his friends" (Jn 15:9,13). Jesus has shown himself truly our friend in giving his life for us on the cross. And he has shown himself our friend by revealing to us all the secrets of his heart. "I have called you friends, because I have made known to you all that I heard from my Father" (Jn 15:15).

And what has he heard from his Father? He has heard not just words to be passed on to us. He has experienced his Father's love for him and has been sent to bring that love to us. "As the Father has loved me, so I have loved you" (Jn 15:9). He has heard a word of mission from his Father. "As the Father has sent me, so I have sent you" (Jn 20:21).

The mission itself is a word of love to us, for it is a revelation of God's love for all of us. The good news, the gospel, is communicated to us in the very love which God gives us in sending his Son. The love is the good news. "For God so loved the world that he gave his only Son" (Jn 3:16). The love is revealed and given in his Son's carrying out his mission of love, laying down his life for his friends.

Thus, the gospel is not just words. It is the fact of God's redeeming love working among us, incarnate and manifest in the person and mission of Jesus. The very mission and presence of Jesus are a message of love and communion. It is the good news of friendship between God and man.

This message of love is the secret which Jesus has heard in the Father's heart and has shared with his friends.

WORD AND SACRAMENT OF FRIENDSHIP

Though Christ's gospel is not just words but is the very love and friendship which he in his Person brings to us from the Father, he has also expressed this love in words, the words of his Sacred Scriptures. And he has communicated this love to us in the Eucharist, the great sacrament of his love: "This is my body which is given for you; this is the cup of my blood, the blood of the new and eternal covenant."

In the Song of Songs, the bride asks the bridegroom for "the love which is better than wine" (1:2). This is God's own love poured out to us in the cup of the precious blood of Jesus. As servants of this love, we must dwell in this love which we serve. Because we minister the Lord's own love to his people, we have to belong to the Lord in intimate friendship.

The spirituality of every servant and friend of Christ has to be eucharistic, and it has to be rooted in God's word. We have to belong to the Lord in the consecration which is faith, ever listening to his word of love. And we have to belong to him in the consecration which is love, dwelling in his love in eucharistic communion, drinking the love better than wine before administering it to others.

Traditionally, it is the deacon at Mass who passes the chalice of the precious blood to God's people. In a very special way, the diaconate is a ministry of love. Deacons not only minister the precious blood but also the works of love which are the fruit of the precious blood. The ministry to the poor has always been the special charge of deacons. "Deacon," we said, means "servant," servant of Christ's ministry of love and friendship. The deacon, however, is a living symbol of every servant of Christ, every Christian. As an ordained minister of God's people, he is a sacramental sign, which stands not apart from the people, but stands out among them. By living it himself, the deacon witnesses to the reality of Christian love which all must live.

Every true Christian, every friend and servant of Christ, is rooted in faith and fruitful in love. Faith is not simply adherence to God's word. It is surrender to Christ's love. It is dwelling in that love: "If you dwell in me, and my words dwell in you, ask what you will, and you shall have it. This is my Father's glory, that you may bear fruit in plenty and so be my disciples. As the Father has loved me, so I have loved you. Dwell in my love" (Jn 15:7–9).

Faith in his love is expressed especially by participating in the eucharistic sacrament, which infallibly pours out that love into our hearts. Thus, the liturgy of the word, alerting our faith, is completed only in the eucharistic sacrament, for faith in his word is perfected only by dwelling in his eucharistic love. "Whoever eats my flesh and drinks my blood dwells in me and I in him" (Jn 6:56).

Faith is receiving his love, dwelling in it, living this love, acting from it, bringing it to others. This love is a living relationship in which we dwell in Christ and he dwells in us. It is a relationship which is fruitful in spreading this love to others.

LORD IN COVENANT LOVE

The one who calls us friend is our Lord. And the correlative of Lord is servant. But he is a Lord whose kingdom is covenant love. My faith is first of all my personal belonging in love to the person of my Lord, surrendering to his love: "My Lord and my God" (Jn 20:28). But it is a belonging to him within the new and eternal covenant in his blood, and therefore a belonging also to all who are in the covenant.

For the words of my commitment in faith, "My Lord and my God," echo the traditional covenant promise: "I will be their God, and they shall be my people" (Jer 31:33). Jesus too, in his words the morning of his resurrection, echoes the covenant promise when he says: "I am ascending to my Father and your Father, to my God and your God" (Jn 20:17). Thus, he indicates the ratification of the new and eternal covenant in his blood, poured out as he ascends to the Father by way of the cross.

The Lord Jesus exercises his lordship by pouring out the grace of the new covenant. This grace is the life in the Holy Spirit. He ascends to the Father's right hand and receives the Holy Spirit whom he sends into our hearts.

The life in the Holy Spirit is God's own life in us. This life can be lived only as communion with God in communion with one another. The fruit of the blood of the new covenant is God's own love poured out into our hearts through the Holy Spirit who is given to us (Rom 5:5). In him, we are all "knit together in love" (Col 2:2).

Thus Jesus exercises his lordship by bringing men together with God in a communion of loving friendship. Only in real love is the covenant truly effective. Only through this love is Jesus truly Lord. He reigns as king only to the extent that men are united in the communion of love.

We see then why the servants of the Lord must be truly friends of the Lord, themselves living the covenant love. For in no other way can his servants effectively mediate this love to others and advance the Lord's kingdom.

For as ministers of his love, we are ministers of his communion, the communion of men with God and with one another, in the covenant love given to us in the precious blood of Jesus. The service we render as friends of Jesus consists in fostering and mediating the communion of men in covenant love. But Christian mediation is accomplished only by living what one mediates, mediating love in the very living of it. I can bring divine friendship only by being a friend of the Lord and by befriending my fellowmen.

COMMUNITY WITH A MISSION

That is why the Church is community of love and joy before it is mission to the world. Mark defines the apostles as those who are chosen *to be with the Lord* and to be sent forth to preach (Mk 3:14). They must be with the Lord, sharing his own life in the communion of friendship. Only from this communion with Christ in communion with one another are they sent forth to preach.

This is true of the whole Church. The Church is much more than mission and service to the world. The Church is first of all a community of friendship with Christ. Her mission springs from the communion of friendship to bring others into this communion. Her mission is to mediate divine friendship to all mankind; and this mission can be fulfilled only by living in friendship with the Lord and with one another, reaching out to embrace more and more persons in this love.

The Church is most herself when she celebrates the sacred liturgy. When she withdraws within herself to celebrate the liturgy, whether it be the Eucharist or morning or evening prayer, she is like a family before its members go out for their day's work, or which is reunited at the end of the day's work. In the liturgy, she allows herself the joy of living her communion with Jesus Christ, in communion with all her children. She already enjoys here and now the presence which she will possess in all its fullness at his second coming. Out of this family life of God's children, in communion with Jesus their brother and God their Father, flows the apostolate to bring others into the same communion of love.

Thus, even before it is the source of the apostolate, eucharistic communion is for the sake of continuing spiritual communion—that is, communion with God in the unceasing prayer of friendship with the Father in the Holy Spirit of his Son. It is loving communion with the Lord, who calls us not merely servants, functionaries in carrying out his work and doing his will, but friends, sons and daughters whose highest calling is to find sheer joy in loving communion with God, children who are at leisure in their Father's house, delighting in his presence, finding joy just in being with him, giving thanks for his great glory.

Only out of this fullness of friendship with God and friendship with our immediate community springs our ministry of love and friendship to all our fellowmen. Since the gospel we mediate is not just words but the very reality of Christ's love, our mediation, our ministry of love, is this love operative in our own persons, uniting us with the Lord and with the Lord's people. This love springs from one source: the Lord's heart and our hearts in which the Lord dwells. Our hearts and his are one. This love reaches out to embrace all others in this loving friendship.

For when Jesus said, "Do this in memory of me," he was speaking not only of the eucharistic celebration itself. He was speaking of the love he had shown in laying down his life for us. "Do this in memory of me" means "Love in the way that I loved, with the very love which I pour out to you in my eucharistic blood. There is no greater love than this, that a man should lay down his life for his friends." Therefore, "Do this in memory of me" means "By the power of the Eucharist, love one another as I have loved you." We minister Christ's love to others only by living it ourselves, loving as he loved, with his own love.

Jesus taught this truth by doing it. He was servant in washing his disciples' feet, symbolizing how he washes us all in his blood. "If I, your Lord and Master, have washed your feet, you also ought to wash one another's feet. I have set you an example; you are to do as I have done for you" (Jn 13:14). Do this in memory of me; that is, serve one another by the power of the love I communicate to you in my eucharistic blood.

The self-sacrifice involved in the Christian ministry is a way of continuing the Lord's own sacrifice. The very carrying out of the mission of love is a laying down of one's life with Jesus. We can minister his love only by actually loving in the way he loved.

THE CONSECRATION OF HUMAN LOVE

The Lord's love, effective in our hearts, redeems and sanctifies our human love. It brings all human love to perfection in the covenant love. Christ came to redeem and sanctify all human love, for he came to redeem human life and all the human relationships in which this life is lived. Jesus remains forever human, even though he is forever Lord God. As Lord, he reconciles humankind with God and with one another in universal brotherly love and friendship.

This love and friendship have to be expressed concretely in all human relationships: conjugal, familial, community, civil, social, cultural, international. Such is God's will, his saving will. He wills to save us in a communion of brothers and sisters, children of God.

As minister of God's love and friendship, the Christian needs to discern how this saving will of God is to be carried out in the concrete details of daily life. Salvation consists in living God's life, in true love, in every life situation. For God wills to save us in our daily circumstances, through our carrying out of his covenant will that we love one another. Both the word of love we listen to in the liturgy and the love better than wine which we drink in the precious blood must be put into effect in everyday living. Therefore, we must be expert in faith's discernment. Faith's discernment is the ability to see, in the light of God's word, how to live the faith in everyday life.

But to live the faith is to dwell in Christ's love, living in his love, acting from that love, spreading it, and building it into universal friendship. "This is his one commandment: that we should believe in the name of his Son Jesus Christ, and love one another" (1 Jn 3:23). This is the Christian ministry in which all

Christians share. We must discern in faith how to live in love, how to express our covenant love by doing always whatever promotes God's friendship among men. This discernment is possible only if we dwell in Jesus and his words dwell in us (Jn 15:7ff.).

To discern his will, then, means to discern in every life situation, in the light of his word, whatever fosters love and brotherhood in the fullness of justice.

First, if the Christian is married, he or she, or better, the two together, must discern, in the light of God's word, how to carry on the mission of divine love and communion in their own family. This is their first responsibility before God. Divine love and friendship, we said, can be mediated to others only by living it. But it cannot be lived alone. It can be lived only with others, and the married person lives it first of all with his family.

Because Christian love is Christ's own love poured out into our hearts in the eucharistic sacrifice, Christian love by its very nature tends toward self-sacrifice for the good of others. St. Paul expresses it thus: "Live in love as Christ loved you, and gave himself up on your behalf as an offering and sacrifice whose fragrance is pleasing to God" (Eph 5:1). A few lines later, Paul expresses a very specific way of living Christ's self-sacrificing love, when he says to husbands and wives: "Husbands, love your wives as Christ loved the Church and gave himself up for it, to consecrate it. . . . Wives, be subject to your husbands as to the Lord" (Eph 5:25, 22).

In other words, the Christian marriage covenant is a concrete way of living the new covenant in the blood of Christ, a way of sacrificing self in love for others.

The Christian's family life is not a compartment of life sealed off from his service in the Church and world. Rather, it is his first area of ministry of the communion and love which is the fruit of the word and of the Eucharist. He so nurtures Christian love and friendship in his own family that the family, living this divine communion in a wonderful fullness, mediates it to others.

THE OPEN WE

The love and friendship which Jesus establishes among men by the grace of the new covenant are like a great web of love in which a multitude of men and women and children are woven together. In a woven fabric each link is closest to the links immediately next to it, and yet is united through them with all the other links. So, in the web of love embodying the grace of the covenant in Christ's blood, I love first of all, in a more intimate way, those who are closest to me.

Thus, the married person will love first of all his wife and family. However, the "we" which he forms with his wife in love is an open "we," open in love to all whom they can embrace: their children, their neighbors, and all to whom their ministry of love and friendship can reach out. The Christian's wife will support him in this ministry, because in love for him she will want him to be his truest self, faithful to his vocation as minister of Christ's friendship. This means she will want him to be all that he can be for others.

The covenant of Jesus is open to all mankind. It is never closed in upon itself. It is a mediation of love and communion to all. Out of the joy of love and friendship in the home springs the ministry which nurtures the joy of Christian friendship, as well as the ministry to the sorrowing and the needy, to the ignorant and to the morally weak.

Jesus can say of each married Christian, as he said of Zacchaeus, "Today salvation has come to this house" (Lk 19:9). And not just to the house, but to the whole community. For Zacchaeus was an official, deeply involved in the daily life of his town. When he was converted to Jesus, Jesus did not require him to give up his livelihood as a tax collector, but did require that he live it in justice and love. That is what Zacchaeus began to do immediately. "Behold, Lord," he says, "the half of my goods I give to the poor; and if I have defrauded anyone of anything, I restore it fourfold" (Lk 19:8). He administers his property not just for the benefit of himself and his family, but for the good of the poor and needy as well.

So too every Christian, as a minister of Christian love, ministers this love not only in his family, but in his work and in his business, expressing his love by doing only what is right and just, and doing what he can to make his office or factory a Christian community, mediating love and friendship to others. All his work is a service of love.

To show that all human activity should be a service of love in Christ, Yves Congar writes: "You should not say of a shoemaker that he makes shoes, but that he keeps Christians shod. . . . 'To make shoes' refers only to production and implies that the maker's only aim is his personal profit." But one's craft or one's profession, and all the goods and property produced and acquired by it, have a purpose beyond all personal advantage. Everything is a service; everything is a ministry.

In the French language in which Fr. Congar wrote, the word for craft or trade or profession is *metier*. The word *metier* evolved from the Latin *ministerium*, ministry or service. Every human work is a ministry or service, and it ought to be rendered in love and communion. All human life and work should find its consummation and fulfillment in this love and communion.

Christian ministry, whether in doing one's daily work or in ministering to the aged and the sick, the poor and the oppressed, carries out the command of Jesus, "Do this in memory of me." For participation in the eucharistic sacrifice is complete only in the works of love.

"I have called you friends" because I have commissioned you as my servants to continue my own mission of friendship. I have made you ministers of my love and reconciliation. This love and reconciliation are themselves the Good News, the Gospel, the mystery hidden from before all ages in the heart of God (Eph 3:9), but now revealed to the world in the very love and friendship of those whom Jesus has sent as servants of his love (Eph 3:10).

Jesus will show himself friend to your fellowmen through your love for them. Your love for them will relay the message, "You are my friends," spoken to them by his love in laying down his life for them. For his own love is present and active in your love, drawing your fellowmen together into his friendship. Christ is present in the reality of the love he is forming in your hearts, he is present in his love in you which binds you together among yourselves and with all those whom you love, he is present in your love reaching out to others.

Your love is an effective revelation of God's love for the world, because it is an active presence of God's love. You will communicate Christ's message of love in the way he did—by living it.

You will carry on your ministry so that your own joy in Christ will be full. According to John, that is the motive for every ministry: to bring others into communion with God so that one's own joy in this communion will be complete. John writes: "What we have seen and heard we proclaim to you, so that you may have communion with us; and our communion is with the Father and with his Son Jesus Christ. And we are writing this so that our joy may be complete" (1 Jn 1:3–4).

The joy you find in friendship with God will be complete only when you bring all whom you can into this same friendship.

TWO

WE WERE MEANT TO BE KNOWN

God does not love us because we are good. We are good because God loves us. His love makes us good by drawing to full development the potentialities which he himself has lovingly created in us. Each one of us is a wonderful mystery of his love. Each one is very special. Each is endowed with potentialities beyond imagining. Most of us do not live even a fraction of the marvelous potentiality that God has given us.

A painter expresses his creation on canvas, a poet puts his creation into words and onto paper, even if he does not show it to anyone. But his work does not reach the fullness of its being, except in appreciation by others. The fullness of every creation is to be known, to be appreciated.

The wonderful mystery which is you is not complete until you are appreciated. God has created you as a beautiful masterpiece, a hidden mystery which is not yet fully revealed. The fullness of your mystery does not come into being until you are known and lovingly appreciated.

It is only in the mystery of appreciation that your potentialities come into full being. Appreciation is the sun which draws forth into blossom and fruitfulness what existed before only as a seed. There are things in us which we do not even know are there until they are drawn forth by someone's love for us. We all fear to try something. How would we know then that we have these talents or qualities if we never try to do anything? We fear rejection, we do not want to fail, so we try nothing and therefore never get to know our powers. We need someone's loving appreciation to encourage us.

Without appreciation, God's fullness in us could never grow, because it would be held back by fear. All the talents we have which are meant to glorify him would never reach actuality because of our fear of failure. Appreciation gives us courage. God's glory will never be realized except under the sun of appreciation which brings our powers to life.

Therefore the deepest desire of our being is to be known, because only in being fully known and lovingly appreciated can we fully be. The whole thrust of our being is to be appreciated. Which is to say that we are meant to glorify the Lord! The fullness of our being is meant to be praise, to be a glory to God.

God is not fully glorified for what he has done in you until someone like me appreciates you, and praises God for you, and thanks him for the wonders he has done in making you the beautiful creature you are. I am glorifying God just in appreciating you as a masterpiece of God's love.

But only in loving you can I fully savor the beauty God has put in you. Only in loving you can I know you fully and rightfully esteem you. For only the eyes of love can see your full beauty.

Only loving appreciation can draw out your full beauty. Beauty, they say, is in the eyes of the beholder. More than that, beauty is somehow created by the loving beholder, for loving appreciation makes the loved one blossom forth in greater beauty. In appreciating you in loving friendship, I am helping you to become more beautiful. My love for you, like God's, is creative. It draws out the best in you.

When all your beauty is seen as the work of God's love, when I love you truly in the Lord, the whole focus of my appreciation of you is really appreciation of the Lord. My loving appreciation of you redounds to the glory of the Holy Trinity.

The misery of not being appreciated is the misery of being the victim of a lie. Why is this? Because the truth is that we *are* beautiful; we are all God's masterpieces. The lie is that people treat me as if I were not a masterpiece. This is an untruth. It is an insult to the Lord to ignore the beauty in me. The fullness of the masterpiece is achieved only in the recognition of the truth, "This is worthy of appreciation!" But it is not enough to recognize the truth. The recognition must be voiced in words and signs of appreciation. That is why Paul can tell us that it is right and virtuous to "give honor where honor is due" (Rom 13:7).

This is the whole approach of a good and loving teacher in dealing with her pupils. And they respond to it beautifully. The loving teacher, or mother, believes with all her heart that each person in her charge is a tremendous masterpiece alive with potentialities, and she treats each accordingly. By appreciating them, she frees them to expect great things of themselves because of what God has given them. She appreciates them because it is the truth; they are God's masterpieces. It is a lie when people do not appreciate these young people! All are worthy of appreciation. Love's eye can always detect the latent good, love's warmth can always bring it to fruition.

Appreciation of our fellowmen is intimately related to the contemplation of God. The contemplative eye sees the beauty of God everywhere, and especially in the wonders he is accomplishing in his sons and daughters, his new creation in Christ his Son. Only the eye that is open to this beauty is fully open to God's direct revelation of himself in the interior graces of the heart.

That is why Thomas Aquinas shows the intimate relationship between honor given to fellowmen and praise and worship of God. Honor is but the expression of our appreciation of the goodness and beauty we see in others, just as praise of God is the expression of our appreciation of the wonders we recognize in him. We do not adequately honor and worship God unless we lovingly recognize and appreciate the wonders he is doing in our fellowmen. We do not adequately honor God unless we do all we can to encourage and bring out the goodness and beauty of our fellowmen. And this we can do only in love.

Adoration and praise of God are difficult for one who is characterized by an unwillingness to honor his fellowmen when honor is due them. The failure to honor our fellowman often stems from envy. We see his perfections as threats, for he outshines us and makes us look poor by contrast. So instead of honoring him, rejoicing in his goodness, we are guilty of detraction, pointing out all his defects. Giving honor to our fellowmen and worship to God is a matter of simple truth and justice, of being true to things as they are. The truth of life includes acknowledging and rejoicing in excellence wherever we find it, whether in our parents as the source of our life, in a child's efforts and successes in his schoolwork, in a holy man's virtue, in a scientist's contributions to mankind's well-being. The same truth and justice impel us to praise and rejoice in the goodness and holiness of God.

Only truth in all the relationships of life opens us totally to the truth and love of God. To refuse to honor and rejoice in goodness wherever we find it closes us in around our narrow self, and we are unable to experience love from God or from any other.

Obviously, the spirit of irreverence toward our fellowmen, lack of esteem for them, unwillingness to give recognition where it is deserved, is a great obstacle to prayer and communion with God. He who is selfishly closed in upon himself is not open to the experience of God. The man who is little inclined to honor and encourage his fellowmen has no taste for the praise of God.

True love and friendship always have eyes to see the worth of the loved one, and to enhance this worth by love's admiring appreciation. This ability to love and appreciate a fellowman is closely akin to the love and praise of God. And vice versa: Appreciation and praise of God open us to appreciation of our fellowmen.

The joy of lovingly appreciating those we love and of being lovingly appreciated is the fullness of our being and the completion of our existence somewhat in the way that joyous knowledge and loving appreciation are the fullness of the life of the three divine Persons, who rejoice infinitely in one another.

As persons, we were made for love, we were made for friendship and communion; for a person is complete only in loving relationships with others. Personal relationships consist in knowing and being known, revealing self and being accepted, loving and being loved. That is why I cannot be fully myself until I am known and appreciated in a relationship of loving communion. The fullness of friendship is my overflowing joy in appreciating my loved one's beauty, which I have helped bring to its full perfection by the sun of my appreciation. In the communion of friendship, this process is mutual.

God himself experiences this joy in his creatures. "May the Lord rejoice in his works!" (Ps 104:31). Who alone can fully know us, fully love us, fully appreciate us? To whom alone can we reveal ourselves without fear of rejection? Is it not the Lord, whose persistent word to his creatures is, "Fear not! The Lord is with you!" He loves you; he finds joy in you. But how can one believe that such love is possible, if he has never experienced the love of his fellowmen? That is why God has given us the mission of love and friendship, to bring love where there is no love, and to reveal God's own love for all mankind.

THE NEED FOR INTIMACY

The need to be known is the need for intimacy. Intimacy means being fully at home with someone. Home is not a place. It is where I am fully known and loved and received just as I am. It is where I am free to be completely myself without putting on acts to win another's approval. Only in the presence of my family and my true friends am I at home. Only trusted love can give such intimacy.

Intimacy means letting myself be fully known, without fear of rejection. It means my responding to another's love by showing myself completely, trusting implicitly that the other will love what I show him. It means being fully known and lovingly appreciated.

The complete trust of intimacy is symbolized by the unashamed nakedness of Adam and Eve in their innocence. Their nakedness signified that they were fully at home with God and with each other, trusting completely in one another's love and acceptance. It is the fear of rejection which impels us to hide from one another.

Intimacy is a love which accepts me fully even when it sees that I am far from perfect. It is a love which patiently nurtures in me whatever is imperfect, a love which always sees my potentialities for good and draws them to full blossom by the sun of appreciation.

The fullness of intimacy requires that this appreciation be mutual. I must appreciate the love and the appreciation that are nurturing me. I must respond by striving to be ever more worthy of that appreciation, trying to please the one who loves me, growing into the goodness and beauty which will give him joy.

Only intimacy, that is, being at home in the love of others for me, fulfills my God-given need to be known and accepted. For only intimacy provides the full appreciation that draws forth the best potentialities with which God has endowed me. Only in intimacy can I be my best self. For I was made for love and friendship and am therefore my best self only in the intimate communion of love and friendship. Only when I am lovingly appreciated and respond to that appreciation by becoming my best self, thus giving joy to those who love me, can I fulfill my God-given need to be known and loved.

The need to be known and lovingly appreciated in intimacy is simultaneously the need to give joy to the Lord. It is the need to be beautiful, perfect, appreciated for the glory of God. Thus, in loving appreciation of those who love me, I strive to please not just my human friends, but I strive above all to give joy to my heavenly Father, so that, like Jesus, I can truthfully say, "I do always what pleases him" (Jn 8:29).

In the intimacy of friendship, I gradually become aware of my selfishness, my sinfulness. The requirements of intimacy are certain to show up my weaknesses. For example, in the warmth of another's loving acceptance of me, I gradually become aware of how ungrateful I tend to be, how I tend to take the other's love and appreciation too much for granted. I may even begin to realize that I have been demanding to be accepted without my making the effort to become more worthy of acceptance. I have not been mending my ways so that I might give joy to those who love me by acquiring the goodness which their love desires for me.

Gradually it dawns on me that the greatest motive for self-improvement is my love's desire to give joy to those who love me, especially to God, who loves me as no one else does. I give them joy by becoming the true self which their unselfish love wants me to be. Through the experience of a friend's love for me, I begin to realize God's intimate love for me; I come to believe that he finds joy in my beauty and perfection. This realization becomes a powerful inspiration for desiring to be faithful to him.

The desire to be known and lovingly appreciated, then, the thrust toward becoming good and beautiful to please those who love me, is very good, for it is meant to be fulfilled in love's continuing endeavor to give joy to the ones who love me. It should not be feared or discouraged.

Certainly we must avoid sinful ways of trying to please others: flattery, boasting, exerting power or display to win attention, obsequiousness (which can even go to the extent of letting another abuse me because I fear to lose his love). Sinful ways of pleasing others are all abuses of love and friendship, for they are abuses of the God-given desire to be worthy of loving attention and appreciation.

The frustrated desire for loving attention and appreciation can lead even to great crimes. Men have highjacked airliners, shot down scores of their fellowmen, committed other atrocious crimes, to satisfy in some way their need for attention. This fact shows how desperately our world needs the apostolate of love and friendship and loving appreciation.

The fact that the desire to be pleasing to others is so much abused is no reason for killing this desire by a false humility. The God-given desire to please and give joy to those who love us can be brought to authentic fulfillment only when we please them by authentic love and goodness.

FREEDOM FROM SELF-PREOCCUPATION

Only when I have been deeply known by someone who has not rejected me am I freed from the fear of rejection. If I have never experienced the warmth of love, I am filled with fears of rejection, thinking I am not lovable. Only the experience of friendship can free me from these fears and from excessive preoccupation with self. For until I have experienced loving friendship, subconsciously I am constantly worried about myself, fearing that I am nothing, nothing worthy of love and attention. And indeed, as a creature who really am nothing sheerly of myself, this fear is well-founded. It results from my experience of my creaturely helplessness. Only love and appreciation can bring me out of this nothingness and out of my fear of worthlessness and rejection.

Only when I am loved deeply by someone who does not reject me can I assume that I will not be rejected when I go out to other people and try to be at home with them. My friend's love has freed me from the fear of rejection, and therefore it has freed me to love others. It has freed me to be myself, it has called forth the development of my potentialities for love.

Paradoxically, then, the loving attention paid to me in true friendship, far from making me self-centered, frees me from self-centered preoccupation, frees me from the need of paying attention to myself, frees me from the self-consciousness which is ever worrying about whether or not I am lovable. For as long as

I am not sure that I am lovable, then even without knowing it, I am self-conscious, tied up by my own fears. I am not free to love.

Therefore, if a person loves me, he frees me from all of those self-conscious preoccupations of which I may not even have been consciously aware. I no longer have to worry about whether or not I am lovable, because the friendship has proved to me that I am lovable. A person who pays loving attention to me in friendship frees me from the self-consciousness which paralyzes my ability to go out to others in love and hampers even my ability to approach God. The intimacy of friendship frees me not only for God's love; it frees me to love everybody.

Thus, under the influence of another's love for me, I am freed from the self-consciousness of wanting to be pleasing to others, and all the energies of my love can now go outward in giving to others. When I am fully loving others unselfconsciously in this way, then at last I am fully lovable, and I can find joy in giving joy to others by loving them.

THREE

THE FRIENDSHIP OF CATHERINE AND RAYMOND

The very deep friendship in Christ which should characterize the entire Christian community is possible only through an interconnecting web of special friendships inspired by special faith and expressed in special love.

St. Catherine of Siena and Bl. Raymond of Capua loved each other with an intimate and special love. This love, Catherine tells Raymond in a letter, results from a special faith they have concerning each other. This is a divine faith intimately connected with faith in God, for it stems from charity. Catherine says to Raymond:

> Just as love for neighbor proceeds from love for God, so does faith concerning creatures proceed from this love, whether it be general faith or special faith. As there is a general faith corresponding to the love which we ought to feel in general to every creature, so there is a special faith belonging to those who love one another more intimately, like the faith which has established a close particular love between us two.[1]

Failure in this special faith, says Catherine, is a sign of imperfect love of God and neighbor. Clearly, in Catherine's thinking, the special faith uniting her and Raymond in intimate love is an expression of the same theological faith and charity in which they believe in God and love him. "That special faith results in so much love that it cannot believe or imagine that either one of us could wish anything else than the other's good. And it believes earnestly, for it seeks this good with great insistence in the sight of God and men, seeking ever in the other the glory of God's name and the profit of his soul."[2]

If this special faith gives rise to special love, this love in turn has faith that it can do all things for the beloved, hoping and obtaining for him from God all that he needs. "For with the love with which I love myself, with that I love you, in the lively faith that all which is lacking on your part God will complete by his goodness."[3]

SPECIAL FAITH AND THE COMMUNION OF SAINTS

Catherine of Siena is a Doctor of the Church, and so we can trust that her ideas concerning special faith are sound. Indeed, this special faith is a very explicit and concrete manner of putting into action Christian faith in the Communion of Saints.

Christian faith in Jesus Christ, Son of God and savior of the world, is simultaneously faith in the whole economy of salvation, the total mystery of Christ. It is faith in Christ continuing his work of salvation through the members of his Body, the Church, the Communion of Saints. It is faith in the truth that God wills to save us through our special love for one another.

My faith in this general truth needs to be made specific and effective in my faith's conviction that God wills to save me through some specific person, or persons, or groups of persons, to whose love he has specially entrusted me. Thus, he wills to save me through my parents or my wife, through my pastor and my parish community, through the religious community to which he calls me, through the prayers and sacrifices of some cloistered nun, or through some close friend who supports me lovingly in my life in the Holy Spirit.

Likewise, my faith in the Communion of Saints must be made concrete and effective in my conviction that God wills to save someone, or several, or many through me. One must be convinced in faith that he has given someone, or several, or many in a special way to my love. God will not save everyone through me, but he wills to save at least some through me, depending upon the greatness of my heart.

In other words, I can live my general faith in the Communion of Saints only in a concrete, specific way. This faith and my love for all men must not remain inactive and ineffective because it is too vague and general. If I say I love everyone and do nothing more about it, then in reality I love no one. I need special faith which focuses on those whom the Lord has entrusted to my special love. In lively faith I must be convinced that I myself can be saved only by helping to save these by my love for them. When the time comes for me to go to the Father in heaven, I have to be able to say, as Jesus himself did the night before he died, "Father, I have lost none of those whom you have given me" (Jn 17:11). Likewise, I must have special faith in those to whose love I have been entrusted, letting myself be helped by them.

SPECIAL FAITH AND BAPTISM

Special faith is a necessary response to my baptismal grace and commitment. Baptism, incorporating me into the Body of Christ, gives me a share in the redemptive mission of the Church, not just some vague general share, but my own specific, concrete way of carrying out that mission. Thus, my general faith and grace of baptism need to be perfected and made specific by the grace of my personal vocation, which calls me and directs me to my specific mission, entrusting to me the specific persons whom God has given to me to love and save.

There is a profound sense in which all faith is special faith, for my faith is first of all faith in myself; that is, my faith in Christ is first of all the conviction that he died for me personally. I believe not only in God and in Jesus Christ, his only Son, our Lord, and in the sanctifying Spirit; I believe at the same time in myself as loved and redeemed and sanctified by these three divine Persons. In the conviction of my personal grace of faith, my intimate personal call from God, I say with Paul, "I live by faith in the Son of God who loved me and gave himself for *me*" (Gal 2:20).

He called me personally into his mystical body, there to be loved and brought to salvation in the Communion of Saints, the mystical womb of Mother Church.

Thus in a way I myself am an object of my Christian faith. I believe with divine faith that I personally have been called into Christ, into the whole Christ, his mystical body.

Likewise, the Holy Catholic Church, the mystical body, is an object of that same faith. I believe that this Communion of Saints, this Body of Christ into which I am personally called by God, is the source of my salvation, for Christ wills to save me by entrusting me to the love of his chosen ones.

But the same faith and baptism which confide me to this love of others for me entrust me with a responsibility also to love, and not just in an ineffective general way. My specific vocation in the Church will manifest to me which persons the Lord has given me, confiding them to my special faith and love.

In other words, there has to be the concrete, real gift of self to God by the total gift of self for the salvation of some specific person or persons or group of persons, such as my wife or my family, my religious community and those whom God wills to save in and through that community, or some class of needy ones, such as the sick and dying to whom I am dedicated as a doctor or a nurse.

THE ORDER OF CHARITY

How am I to know which persons God has specially entrusted to my love? Rudolf Bultmann writes, "Man loves to choose for himself the object of his love, whereas the divine precept of love signifies that I must love the neighbor whom God places perchance in my way. Then my love becomes obedience."[4] If you love only those who love you, says Jesus, you do no more than the pagans (Mt 5:47).

Every Christian soon discovers, however, that the needy ones who cry out for his love and help seemingly are infinitely numerous. He does not have enough alms to go around to help all those who present themselves in his path, he does not have time and strength enough to devote himself in love to every needy one of whom he is aware. The physical and spiritual neediness in the world about him is endless. Should he then give up, in the hopelessness of not knowing where to start or whom to love?

He must realize in humility that his love, which desires to love everyone, has its limitations, and he must make a choice of whom he is going to love specially; otherwise he will end up loving no one. In making his choice he is guided by the so-called order of charity outlined by Thomas Aquinas, who was so keenly aware that Christian love to be effective has to focus on specific persons, to be loved in specific actions.[5]

The first principle in making this choice is the truth that God has entrusted some to me to be loved and cared for in a special way. That is the very nature of the Christian community, the mystical body, in which each one has his unique vocation, his special role. Therefore, I am obliged to love first of all and above all those who are immediately dependent upon me in the mystical body, and those upon whom I am dependent. Thus, I must have a special love for my parents, my wife, my children, my relatives.

Or, if I am a religious, I must not love just those whom I choose to love, but all those whom God has given me to love as brothers and sisters by calling them into the same religious family. And I must love those whom God wills to save in and through the community to which he calls me. This I do in a practical way by cooperating in love with my religious brothers or sisters to make my community effective both in its internal life of love and friendship and in its apostolic work.

The order of charity, however, is not quite as simple as this. There is a second principle to be applied in making the choice of those upon whom I am especially going to focus my loving action. Since I cannot do everything, I must choose to help and love those most desperately in need. But even this principle must be applied in harmony with the first principle, which obliges me to love specially those closest to me because of my vocation. I do not abandon my family to labor for the poor in far-off India. I do not desert my religious community and its God-given apostolate to engage in another apostolate of my own choosing, no matter how worthy an apostolate it may be.

It is beyond our purpose here to examine the order of charity in detail. We wish merely to recall that there is such an order of love which ensures that my love will fulfill its basic responsibilities, lest in helping Peter I deprive Paul. Love, of course, never limits itself merely to basic responsibilities. Truly generous love soon discovers that it can do far more than it ever dreamed possible. It can fulfill its fundamental obligations and an enormous amount besides. The only thing than can really hinder it is timid selfishness.

SPECIAL FAITH AS A CHARISM

Sometimes the one I am to love with special faith is manifested to me by an unusual charismatic grace, as was the case of St. Jane Frances and St. Francis de Sales. In answer to Jane's prayers for a spiritual guide, Francis was shown to her in a vision, so that later on when she actually met him for the first time, she recognized him as the one to whose love God had entrusted her. A close bond of affection sprang up between these two, facilitating the divine work they were to carry out together.

The special faith and love between persons like Francis and Jane and between Catherine and Raymond were charismatic in the sense that these friends were a gift of God to his Church, and their love was fruitful far beyond the mutual personal sanctification of the two involved. A charism by definition is a grace granted for the common good of the Christian community (1 Cor 12:7). The special attraction of grace between Jane and Francis was fruitful in the establishment of the Nuns of the Visitation, who for three and a half centuries have been enriching the mystical body of Christ. The charismatic graces which brought these saints together pertained, of course, to their grace of vocation, directing their general baptismal mission of love into very specific channels.

A SPECIAL COVENANT OF LOVE

Every special faith and love are concrete expressions of the new and eternal covenant in Christ's blood, into which each Christian enters by faith and baptism. I can live the new covenant of Christian love only if I make it concrete in specific love, focusing my charity first of all on those whom God has given me to love. For, as we have seen, my covenant with Christ obliges me to love my fellowmen not in an abstract way as an indeterminate mass of humanity but as definite, concrete persons. I embody my covenant of love with Christ and his whole people by loving those specific persons whom God puts in my way to be loved by me. Thus, all authentic Christian love is a concrete expression of the new covenant in Christ's blood.

But this is true with special vividness when two people, or a group of people, see one another as specifically chosen by Christ to continue his own work in some great way: for example, those who bind themselves together in love as a religious order. Religious profession in such a community is a way of making one's baptismal share in the new covenant very concrete and effective in community and apostolic love.

In the same way, Christian married people should see their love for each other as a concrete embodiment of the covenant of love between Christ and his Church. Their love for each other is their principal way of making effective their covenant of love with all of God's people.

When two people like St. Catherine and Bl. Raymond are drawn together in special faith and love by a charismatic grace, their love for each other becomes an especially remarkable embodiment of the covenant in Christ's blood. Within the great covenant, the two make a special covenant to work as one in mutual self-giving for the advance of Christ's work of salvation.

Catherine's special faith concerning Raymond saw him as a vessel of election in continuing the Lord's work and saw herself as called to be one with him in this mission, backing him up by offering herself to God as one sacrifice in Christ for the success of his work. By her God-given faith in Raymond as God's chosen instrument, she was animated with love for him and greatly strengthened in her self-giving for his benefit.

Rightly, then, she could call upon him in turn to have faith in her love for him. Once when Raymond failed in a mission, Catherine chided him because he tried to excuse his failure by thinking that her love for him had let him down. Catherine tells him that it was really his own cowardice which was the cause of the failure. "You doubted me, thinking that my affectionate love for you was diminished. . . . In reality my love for you is increased. . . . I shall not stop working for you. . . . Whenever your faults are shown to you, rejoice, and thank the divine goodness which has assigned someone to labor over you, who watches for you in his sight."[6]

And yet because Raymond had proved to be so weak, Catherine felt that perhaps she had let him down in some way by not being heroic enough in her self-offering for him. Raymond's failings were somehow her own, because she and he had become as one in their mutual faith and love. Therefore, she appeals to him to join her in renewing their special covenant in the blood of the new covenant. "My very dear father, I beg of you to pray insistently that you and I together will bathe ourselves in the blood of the humble Lamb, which will make us strong and faithful."[7]

Catherine did not let herself be unduly discouraged by Raymond's failure in his mission and his lack of faith in her love for him. "I keep myself in peace, because I am certain that nothing happens without the mysterious design of God."[8] She could only intensify her offering of self to God for Raymond.

Little did she realize that later God would make her covenant with Raymond fruitful in a far more marvelous way. In her last letter to Raymond before her death, Catherine describes what we might call her last agony, though it took place some weeks before her actual death. In the midst of intense suffering over the miserable state of the Church, she cried out in this agony, "O Eternal God, receive the sacrifice of my life for the mystical body holy Church." The sacrifice was immediately accepted, and she suffered excruciating pain.

When she recovered enough to write about this to Raymond, she told him how her self-offering for the Church was simultaneously an offering for him and for his mission, and for the renewal of the Dominican Order.

A few weeks later, at the very moment when Catherine was dying in Rome, Raymond was in Genoa kneeling before the statue of the Blessed Virgin. He was about to leave for Bologna to attend the general chapter which would elect him head of the Dominican Order. At the moment Catherine died, Raymond heard her voice saying to him very clearly several times, "Do not be afraid! I am with you!"

She was with him after death as she had been with him in life, but now even more effectively than before. As master general of the Dominican Order, aided from heaven by Catherine, Raymond did so much for the renewal and restoration of the Order that he has justly been called the second St. Dominic.

SPECIAL FAITH AND WARM HUMAN AFFECTION

Special faith in each other such as existed between Catherine and Raymond practically demands a deep human affection between the two. Warmth of affection is an integral element of their special bond in divine love. The two are truly "knit together in love" (Col 2:2). One who sacrifices herself as completely as Catherine did for Raymond can hardly help but love him warmly and humanly, and he cannot help loving warmly in return, if he gratefully appreciates her love. The depth of Catherine's affection for Raymond was manifested in her copious tears when she said good-bye to him at St. Paul's Outside the Walls as he set out on a journey.

St. Francis de Sales frankly admitted that he had a deep human affection for St. Jane Frances. "I am ever yours in Jesus Christ, and I marvel at this growth of affection. . . . Why do we think God has willed to make one sole heart out of our two, except that this one heart might be extraordinarily bold, brave, spirited, constant and loving in its Creator and in its Savior?"[9]

He writes to her again, "I feel with ever-increasing force the reality of the union of our hearts, which will truly keep me from ever forgetting you until after, and long after, I have forgotten myself to fasten myself so much the better to the cross."[10] His heart, he tells her, rejoices in her heart as in itself.[11]

Because of the deeply human warmth of his character, Francis could scarcely have escaped noticing the womanly charm of Jane. One day early in their friendship when she was still a young widow, Francis saw her much better dressed than usual and said to her, "My lady, do you wish to marry again?" "No indeed," she replied. "Very well," the bishop said with a smile, "but then you should pull down your flag." She took the hint.

Because God had given Jane to him to be loved with a special faith, Francis could love her warmly and humanly and yet with complete celibate purity, in the way St. Joseph must have loved the virgin Mary, as one given to him by God to be loved: "Joseph, son of David, do not fear to take Mary your wife" (Mt 1:20). Because the love of Francis and Jane was a love of emotionally mature persons, and because they were both completely faithful to their consecration to God, they could love each other with real human affection and still remain celibate. They wanted nothing from their love but God's glory and their own mutual holiness. "I am going to try to keep you ever exalted on the throne which God has given you in my heart, a throne based upon the cross," he writes to her.[12]

Then there is the beautiful love of the two Dominicans, Bl. Diana and Bl. Jordan, St. Dominic's successor. The letters Jordan wrote to Diana have been famous literature for over seven centuries.[13] Jordan writes to Diana, "I do not require your love fully, of that I am deeply convinced. You love me more than I love you. But I cannot bear you to be so afflicted and distressed in mind by reason of this love of yours which is so precious to me."

Because Jordan and Diana, Francis and Jane, Catherine and Raymond were totally consecrated to the person of Christ and to his work of salvation, their hearts were capable of knitting together in a greatly increased love of their fellowmen. United as one in love, they succeeded in loving a multitude of their fellowmen and working together effectively for their salvation.

Such is the freedom and the fruit of celibate love. Francis wrote to Jane: "This then is the bond that unites us, these are the ties that hold us together, and the closer they draw us, the more ease and freedom they will give us. Know, then, that I hold myself closely bound to you, and seek to know no more, save that this bond is not incompatible with other bonds, whether of vow or of marriage."[14]

Every one of us needs someone, or some ones, with whom we can have a mutual special faith and love. For if others need me and are entrusted to my faith and love, at the same time I am very much in need of others and have been entrusted to their love for me. If my faith and love are to be effective to the maximum in helping others, they have to be lived in mutuality with the faith and love of others in regard to me. For I am being saved by others even while I am saving others. I am upheld in my salvation work by others who are loving me, praying and sacrificing for me, and giving me the human love and encouragement I need.

Thus, for example, I am upheld by wife and family even while I uphold them, or I am supported by my religious community even while I support them, or if I am a priest, I am sustained by the sacramental brotherhood of the presbyterate at the same time that I am an aid to them in their personal sanctification and in their apostolate.

But I am especially blessed if God gives me a very close friendship with some specific person who is filled with the grace of God and divine love, and who has received a special faith, hope, and love for me. With such a one I can make a special covenant by which we intensify our participation in the new covenant in the blood of Christ.

HOPE IN MY FRIEND'S LOVE

If I have such a God-given special friendship, I can have a true divine faith and hope in this love which is so concerned about me. I can say to the one who loves me, who sees me in special faith as entrusted to him, "I believe in you, I hope in you, I love you." To the degree that our friendship is authentic divine charity, this special faith, hope, and love are a participation in our theological faith, hope, and charity toward God.

For the love which my God-given friend has for me is itself an act of special faith focused upon me, a faith and love which see me personally as loved and redeemed and called by Christ, or see me as a chosen instrument of God, such as a priest or missionary or leader of a community. This special love for me hopes to obtain for me from God all that I need for my growth in holiness and for my faithfulness in my mission of love. I can have hope in my friend's hope for me, because his love for me springs from his divine hope for my salvation.

Paul tells us that faith founds its love of neighbor on the common participation in one hope: "We have heard of your faith in Christ Jesus and of the love you have for all the saints because of the hope of blessings reserved for you in heaven" (Col 1:3–4). Faith in this common hope impels us to involve ourselves in effective love of neighbor. Charity in the Church loves one's fellowmen precisely because they are elect and co-citizens of eternity. Charity carries on the ministry of love which strives to bring everyone into communion in the life of the Holy Trinity.

Faith and hope in another person's love are possible not just in those marvelous cases of charismatic faith and love such as existed between Catherine and Raymond. A man, for example, can have special faith in his wife if she is obviously a woman of extraordinary faith and love for God. Or one can have special faith and hope in his religious community if it still is truly a community of faith, whose members are vividly conscious of their mutual commitment to the salvation of one another. Or a priest can have hope in the love of his fellow priests for him, if his brothers in the presbyterate have the concern for one another which their common sharing in the one priesthood of Christ calls for.

I can truly believe and hope in my friend's love for me, then, to the extent that it is manifestly divine love inspired by God's Holy Spirit. Like Raymond and Catherine, I can have trustworthy signs that the love is so inspired, and that the friend is truly given me by God.

Catherine's special faith in Raymond had its beginnings in her religious obedience. It was the master general of the Dominican Order who placed her under the spiritual direction of Raymond, and therefore in faith she saw Raymond as given to her by God himself, by means of the order to which God's love had entrusted her in calling her.

So, too, Raymond's special faith in Catherine was rooted in his obedience to his assignment, for faith and charity, working always within the Communion of Saints, oblige us to love in a special way those who are in our care. Spiritual direction can be successful only if there are deep love and mutual trust between the parties directing and directed. Under these conditions, the two mutually benefit each other greatly.

NEED FOR SPECIAL FRIENDS

It is important that all of us have special friends within the greater bosom of our religious community, our parish community, our presbyterate, or in whatever other group God has placed us. For a large community can effectively love its members with the special love and support they need only through the mediation of these special loves between individuals or among the members of smaller groups, such as a seminary class or a novitiate. A novice, for example, should be upheld by the closely knit love of his peer group, and likewise should be able to find a close friend in the novice director, who should truly love those in his charge and should inspire a spirit of loving unity among them.

Likewise, members of apostolic teams should be bound together in deep ties of friendship. Therefore, St. Gregory the Great indicates that no one should be sent out on apostolic work unless he is capable of true love for his fellow workers: "Dear brothers, our Lord sends his disciples to preach two by two. In doing so, he silently indicates to us that should anyone not love his neighbor, he should by no means take upon himself the office of preaching."

The Christian community's love, backing up the preacher, is tangibly and effectively made present with him through the special love of his preaching partner.

KNIT TOGETHER IN LOVE

Paul says that the whole Christian community should be "knit together in love" (Col 2:2). But in knitting the whole web of the fabric is formed only when each link in the web is united with those immediately around it, each of which in turn has connections with others. Thus, the entire fabric holds together in love.

In his various letters, Paul indicates that such a web existed among all the Christian communities. He himself was united in love even with Christian churches which had never seen him face to face, through the mediation of his coworkers who loved these communities and who were themselves closely tied with Paul in love.

Paul writes to the Colossians, for example, and to their neighbors the Laodiceans, who are also to read the letter (Col 4:16), rejoicing in the love they have for one another. He has not personally seen this love, he has only heard about it, for the Colossians and Laodiceans "have not seen my face" (2:1). Yet he is intimately knit together with them in love through Epaphras, the missionary Paul had sent to them. "He is a faithful minister of Christ on our behalf and he has made known to us your love in the Spirit" (1:7–8). Hearing that they too are now "God's chosen ones, holy and beloved" (3:12), Paul cannot help but love them also, and pray that their web of love may be strengthened and be filled with understanding and knowledge of the mystery of Christ (2:1–3).

In the same way Epaphroditus is the link between the Philippians and Paul. He was "your messenger and minister to my need" (Phil 2:25). But now I must send him back to you, because "he has been longing for you all, and has been distressed because you heard he was ill" (2:26). Obviously, the longing of Epaphroditus for the Philippians manifests a deeply human affection in which his God-given love for them was clothed.

Likewise, Paul works through Syzygus, "my true yoke-fellow" (4:3), in order to bring together in love the quarreling Evodia and Syntyche.

Such are the smaller links of close affection in the Christian community, by means of which the whole is knit together in love. The very deep friendship in Christ which should characterize the entire Christian community is possible only through an interconnecting web of special friendships inspired by special faith. Maslow points out that the close friendships of mature persons are relatively few in number. Only the immature person is in love with love, and expects I-thou relationships with every member of his community. Each friend should be linked closely with a few others, each of whom is linked with still another few, and thus the whole web of love is closely knit together. The quality and depth of love in the whole fabric of the community are dependent upon the high quality of each individual friendship.

When the friendship is fully inspired by charismatic special faith, it becomes an apostolic covenant in which the friends work for the salvation of others, and thus bring about love among the many.

FOUR

FRIENDSHIP IS TWO PEOPLE GROWING

True love always promotes the growth of the loved one.

Only in loving and being loved do we grow. The purpose of friendship, therefore, is to help two people grow fully into their true selves. Friends draw forth each other's potentialities, bringing each other to all the fullness of their being. If the friendship is not resulting in this, then it is not a real friendship, it is not unselfish love, it is not true concern for the other, it is not letting him be his true self. If the results of the friendship are jealousy and constant bickering and uneasiness and the friends' inability to do their work, then it is not really a friendship. The real friendship will always be resulting in growth for the parties, making them freer, more responsible.

But there are stages in friendship, just as there are stages in the growth of an individual. It is important to be convinced of this, for two reasons: to allay fears which would hinder growth in the friendship, and to forestall a certain kind of presumption which would prevent further growth. Fear prevents growth by not letting us go forward to beyond where we are, and presumption prevents us from going forward because we presume that the friendship is at its peak; we think that this is all there is, we don't open ourselves to the possibility of further development.

PRESUMPTION

It is wisdom to realize at every stage that this is only a lesser stage and never to have the presumption to say, "This is an ultimate experience." We must get into a frame of mind which expects and promotes continuing growth.

To stop at a lesser stage, and not to grow, is regression. If a married couple, for example, stop at sexual expression of their love and think that this is all there is to it, they are going to regress, they are going to get disgusted, they are going to destroy each other instead of promoting each other's growth. Their resting in the lesser goods of their friendship is sloth, failure to make the effort to go beyond the lesser joys of the honeymoon. Love should never stay at a standstill. If it does not go forward, then it slips backward. To rest in the enjoyment of the lesser goods of a friendship is deterioration.

In friendship, then, the attitude should be one of expectation, of openness to ever more, never to close off, either by fear, or by a subtle form of presumption which says, "We have reached the ultimate, what more could there be than this?" There is more! We must not try to recover and relive the same old experiences of friendship in the same way repeatedly. Everything is new! Childhood is good, but if I am thirty years old and try to relive childhood, something is wrong. I have regressed.

FEAR

In friendship, not only must I live in expectation of greater things to come, but I must also avoid fear. Fear prevents growth by keeping me from taking the risks which are involved in loving others. To allay this fear, I must be convinced that friendship does have its imperfect stages and be willing to accept my imperfections without discouragement. The wonderful fullness of friendship to which I aspire in lively expectation can be reached only by steps.

In these stages I experience my human weakness and selfishness which hinder the fullness of friendship. I tend to get greatly discouraged or even disgusted with myself, thinking perhaps that I am un-Christian because my love for my friends is not yet utterly selfless, but is still seeking the fulfillment of my own needs. The fact is, I cannot possibly be utterly giving and totally selfless in love until my needs are being cared for and I am receiving in love what I need. By its very nature as fostering growth, friendship cares for my needs as well as enabling me to give to the other. Love knows how to give. And this is absolutely true of my love for God, which is forever receiving. I cannot be fully open to God's infinite love and generosity until I have accepted my neediness and unlovableness.

I must not be discouraged, thinking I am un-Christian because I have not yet achieved the ideal, any more than a child would be discouraged because he is a child. But I must courageously reach out, as a child reaches out for manhood, yet not straining too hard, like a child who never tries consciously to force his growth.

In my friendships with others, especially with persons of the opposite sex, I must not have too angelic or Manichaean an idea of love's purity. I must accept my sexuality as inseparable from my humanity, and something to be reverenced, not feared. My healthy acceptance of my sexuality minimizes the risks involved in friendships. The reverent acceptance of my body and of my sexuality as a normal part of my humanity, and necessarily operative in my communication with my fellowmen, lessens the risks of abuse of the emotional elements which may come into play in my relationships with my friends.

Thus, if two people in the earlier stages of their friendship experience intense emotional involvement, that is natural. But they might be tempted to cut themselves off from the friendship in fear and therefore destroy any possibility of growing.

But if they are willing to accept emotional involvement as a normal stage in friendship, they will be at home with it and not make too much of it. This stage will pass away as the friends grow into a new stage in which their hearts are knit together on a more deeply spiritual level. This growth from one stage to another does not happen automatically. For example, if the friends rest on the emotional level as though that were the ultimate in their friendship, their relationship, we said, will deteriorate rather than develop. They must strive for the deep spiritual levels and yet not be discouraged if it takes time to grow beyond the initial strong emotional involvement. They have to have a healthy sense of humor about themselves and await growth patiently.

Too often the very ability to grow in Christian love and friendship has been wounded or killed by excessive fear of the risks involved. If in a friendship each person has a profound reverence for the other as belonging to God, and if each is faithful both to God and to the friend, the seemingly excessive emotional captivation will pass, and a more selfless stage will evolve. Nothing that we are experiencing now is the ultimate. If we are faithful to God and to one another, then there is even more yet to come. This thought will allay paralyzing fears. Fear is an even bigger enemy of growth in friendship than is presumption.

What we have said about presumption in human friendship or thinking that our friendship is at its peak and that we have achieved the ultimate experience is true also of friendship with God. If I try to stop at the emotional experiences of prayer, for example, then I am blocking the way. I am not going to grow in contemplative prayer.

I must have boundless faith in God's love. Faith is like getting a new set of eyes. The new set of eyes is this: to realize that in friendship with God, the best is always still to come, to put no limits on God's love and generosity, always to expect more.

In prayer, the experience of friendship with God, there are certain moments of intense communion with God in which I think that this is the fullness of everything I could ever experience. I tend to rest in these experiences, trying to recover them again just as they were. I do not open myself for even deeper experiences by letting go of these lesser ones. This is sloth, resting in the lesser gifts of God, being content with them. But the sin, the presumption, consists in not realizing that these are only lesser gifts. The sin is an unwillingness to believe in God's love which loves me so much that he can put no limits on what his love wants to do for me.

God wants us to expect infinite riches from his generosity, but he wants us at the same time to open ourselves to these riches by emptying ourselves of all else that stands in the way of his full gift of himself. My sin is to not let God be God, to not expect that he could do even more than this for me. "Not letting God be God" means not letting his love be infinitely generous toward me. Because an experience in prayer is the ultimate which I have so far experienced, I tend to say that this is the absolute ultimate; this is all that I expect from God. This, of course, is a form of ingratitude, a failure to appreciate his gifts as a pledge of greater things to come.

Unconsciously, I form my image of what I expect from God according to what I have already experienced, as if this were all that God had to offer me. In other words, I make what I've experienced the measure of who God is. I make myself the criterion, the measure, of what God wills to give me. I box him into a little capsule, limiting his loving generosity by the narrowness of my faith and desire. I cannot make the leap of faith to believe that there are things that I have never experienced and which God means for me to experience. I refuse to believe others who tell me of these greater experiences. I will not accept their witness, which should open my faith and desire for what I had thought unbelievable. I make myself the measure of what is real and is to be given to me.

God is so beyond everything I could ever expect that believing requires those new eyes which never put any limits on what to expect. Faith always expects more, but without knowing what that more is.

At every stage I must realize that, compared to what is meant to come, this stage is only a lesser gift. I must never think that this stage is the ultimate.

THE REVELATION OF MY SINFULNESS

Involvement in friendship brings out the best in me, it encourages my growth. The sun of someone's love for me draws out my potentialities. Love's encouragement, and my response in using my God-given potential, brings me to a new awareness of all the good that is in me. I feel my powers and am eager to put them to full use in giving to others.

But another important stage in friendship, corresponding to my increasing awareness of the good that is in me, is my growing consciousness of my weaknesses and selfishness. Involvement in a vital friendship reveals to me my many subtle forms of sinfulness. Precisely through my relationships with others, the obstacles to the Lord's full possession of me are revealed to me. I would never see these obstacles if I did not cultivate human friendship. It is in relationships with others that we get to know ourselves.

I would never have known my subtle lordship over others, my possessiveness, my desire to hold on to and to manage others, except through my deep relationships with others. By subtle lordship over my friends, I mean that, sinfully. I try to be lord instead of letting the Lord be their Lord and mine. I try to subject my friends to my own desires. I try to bend them to my own idea of what they should be, rather than let them be free to become, and encourage them to become, the true self the Lord meant them to be. I try to fashion them in my own likeness, rather than let the Spirit of the Lord fashion them in the likeness of God.

Or I assert subtle lordship by indulging my tendency to make myself the whole center of attention. As a child, before I grow up, I need to be the center of attention until I acquire self-confidence. At that stage, I almost need to be lord and try to attract attention, so that I can come to be convinced that I am worthy of love and esteem. But once I am convinced of my intrinsic value, then I can and should forget myself and pay attention to others.

Once I have a healthy self-esteem, I can be open to others and love them selflessly, and bring them through the same stages to be open to the Lord.

There will be a natural process of evolution. In my friendships with the Lord and with my fellowmen, I do not have to force one stage to follow another; indeed, I cannot force them. The little girl puts her doll aside after a while, as she grows into the experience of something else which gives her even greater satisfaction. But she has to pass through the earlier stages which will free her to experience those deeper things. So, too, a three-year-old has to be the center of attention. That is good and healthy. But if he is forever seeking attention, if he is thirty years old and still has to be lord, then something is wrong

What at an early stage of my psychological growth was necessary, later on can be sinful, if I continue unduly in this stage, resting in it, indulging in it, when I could have and should have passed on to a better stage. A religious woman, for example, who should have cultivated total attention to the Lord and should have grown up enough to forget herself, sinfully tries to be lord in his place by her flirtatious efforts to be herself the center of attention. Her sincere friendships with others should help her become more conscious of sinful tendencies such as this.

If friends are truthful to one another and faithful to one another, then as their friendship grows, they will increase in sensitivity to their sinful tendencies. They will become more and more sensitive to the subtle forms of lordship which each exercises over or accepts from the other. What in the earlier stages of friendship were needed forms of expression, taking care of the neediness of the friends, will be seen in the later stages as a subtle form of selfish lordship, as sinful holding on to the possessiveness and attention which are no longer necessary.

The sincere and faithful friend will abandon what is no longer needed. What a child needs at three years he will not need at seven; these needs and desires will drop off naturally. The little child who loves dolls and wants to cuddle them will not have to force herself to stop loving to cuddle her dolls, because as she grows, her need and desire for dolls will drop away naturally. So too we need not fear the imperfect "need" stages of friendship. In the honest and healthy growth of a friendship, the imperfect, more self-centered stages will fall away as we grow into the richer stages. We cannot force ourselves to perfection without going through the necessary stages of growth.

The more I become at home with another in friendship, then, the more I get to know myself. In my vital relationships with others, I see myself in operation and become aware of my faults, my sinfulness, as well as my good qualities. It is only in living a relationship that I learn of my sinful tendencies to abuse a relationship. Until these sinful tendencies are unveiled and uprooted, my relationship with God will be hampered by them. By letting myself experience friendships deeply, I have my hidden sins revealed to me, which I would never have known otherwise. In the give-and-take of human relationships, in the friction of repeated encounters which make the sparks fly, I become aware of my rough edges and know what I must polish away. The person who is never involved with others, but withdraws into a shell, never learns either his strengths or his weaknesses.

Thomas Aquinas, with his usual keen psychological insight, long ago pointed out how human relationships thus prepare us for the contemplation of God. He shows how, even more than abstinence and chastity and the virtues which control the bodily appetites, the social virtues, the ones which set us right with our fellowmen, in our relationships with them in love, prepare us for communion with God. It is the virtues which rightly regulate our human relationships in love which most effectively kill in us the selfishness and self-centeredness, which are the obstacles to God's self-revelation to us in contemplative prayer. Deep involvement in a Christian friendship, then, can very effectively reveal to me my sinful tendencies so that I might uproot them—or, rather, destroy them by the unselfishness of the new stage of friendship. I advance to the new stage in dying to my selfishness through peace and reconciliation with my friend.

HONESTY IN FRIENDSHIP

Honesty in facing them is the way to overcome the sinful tendencies which are revealed in the give-and-take of friendship. The devil named is the devil exorcised. When a friend becomes aware of a sinful tendency in himself, he tends to hide it from the other and from himself. The remedy will be honesty, and a healthy sense of humor. We need the humility and the good humor to realize that we are not consummate saints. We must accept our limitations with patience, expecting our growth and improvement to take place in stages.

"Yes, this is where I am." I must face honestly my shortcomings, my sinfulness, my strong desires. I must recognize and admit to myself all my feelings.

There are often desires and feelings that I have which I cannot live out in the way the feelings would carry me. For example, I might feel angry and might feel like tearing someone to shreds. Or I might have sexual feelings which are strong but which I have no right to express. But just because I cannot act out these feelings does not mean I must deny their existence. I must admit them and redirect and sublimate them. I will never achieve the full integration of my person if I deny that I have these human feelings which stem from my very nature and are keys to my human needs.

Only by honestly facing my feelings can I adequately integrate them into the totality of my life. Our feelings are our friends, no matter how shameful or imperfect these feelings may seem to be, no matter how weak I may seem to be in having them. Feelings cannot lie. There is a cause for every feeling we have. Our feelings are our friends because they are the keys to needs that we have.

If we put our feelings out of our mind, if we pretend we do not have them, saying, "I should not feel this way," we are lying to ourselves. The fact is that we do feel this way, and there is a reason for it. It is part of ourselves to feel this way. We must find out why we feel this way, and then we can work toward a solution.

If we face the feelings honestly and are not afraid to speak of them to ourselves and to our friends and to God, then we are on the way toward coming to a solution of our problem and growing to a new stage in which this need has been cared for and integrated into the unity of our personality.

In friendship, we can help one another to overcome our sinful tendencies and to integrate our feelings and our desires into our whole personalities. We must help our friend to overcome his fault by helping him face the truth about himself. To help my friend face his fault, I must courageously be honest in revealing to him my own feelings about his failing. This is such an important point: at every stage of the friendship to have the courage to speak what is inside me.

Suppose, for example, that my friend is at the stage of possessiveness. We all want to cling to "this one" and have him or her as our own. This is a natural enough stage. But there has to be some kind of death to it. I must help my friend overcome it by helping him face the truth about it. I have to be willing to take the risk of my friend's disfavor by speaking my feelings about it. "You are holding on to me too tightly. Give me room to be myself. I need a little distance from you."

My friend has to be willing to do some dying to self and allow me to be. In allowing me to be, he becomes himself. In giving me distance, he has distance to be, too. For he is hampered in his growth if he is excessively dependent upon me.

When I want persons to be my friends and try to make them be my friends and they do not respond the way I want them to, I try to make them respond. I demand things of them. All that does is make them run away. I must become firmly convinced that the only true friendship will be that which is freely given. If others do not respond the way I want them to, they certainly will not do it by my demanding it of them. So I cannot lose by letting them be free and letting them have their distance. There is no way in which I can lose by doing this, and this is the way in which I can gain everything. For either at a distance they will find out how much they love me and will come to me of their own free will, or they will go away. But that is best, because I could not have kept them anyway by my demanding. There is no way I can lose in allowing my friend the freedom to be himself.

All this applies to friendship with God in prayer too. In prayer I cannot be demanding of God. I should simply hold myself ready to receive, with complete trust in his love.

Letting my friend be free is the greatest gift of friendship I can give—the gift of trust. I am really saying, "I trust your love." If I am always demanding attention, it is because I do not believe that you love me. Not letting you be free, because I am afraid you will not come through with your friendship, is an offense to your love.

But love has to pass through that stage, because this possessiveness is only a manifestation of the inability to believe that I am really loved. Possessive stages are simply an indication that the person has not yet been shown sufficiently that he is loved, and therefore he does not believe it. When he is sure of being loved, this possessiveness passes. People cannot grow, they cannot be free to love others, until they have overcome the possessive stage of love. But they cannot overcome this till they have truly experienced genuine love.

Hence, when we are generous in loving and in being a true friend (gently weaning our friend away from possessiveness), we are creating in him the power to love others in turn; we are giving him freedom to love. We have to be generous and patient in loving those who are still immature in loving. For unless they are loved, they will not pass through the various stages of growth and will not grow in the power to be a true friend and to love others in turn.

For there is no flower that has not been brought to bloom by the needed sunshine. There is nothing wrong in going through the stages of being possessive or of being overinvolved emotionally. These are normal stages that we have to go through because we are who we are, and if someone will love us through these stages, they will see the fruit of it. You cannot love a butterfly until you have loved a caterpillar. You have to be willing to love some caterpillars, and to be loved as a caterpillar, knowing that someday we are going to be butterflies.

Each stage of growth will pass, if I have a healthy sense of at-homeness with it. Instead of being afraid of the stage or disgusted with myself because I still have these human weaknesses, first of all I must be truthful and say, "Yes, this is where I am." I must have a kind of gentleness and patience with myself, in hopefulness that this stage too will pass. In the conviction that my imperfect stage will not last forever, I will be free, and always open to growing.

I must learn to be at home with my human nature, and rejoice in being human, grateful that God made me a man or a woman, not a stick or a stone.

PAINS OF FRIENDSHIP

There can be so much happiness in the early stages of my friendship that I tend to think that I need nothing apart from my friend and that I will find in him the fulfillment of all that I long for.

But no human friend can fill the ultimate void in the human heart. Only God can do that. If I expect everything from a friendship, sooner or later I will suffer the pain of disappointment. How often in a marriage, for example, the husband or wife feels trapped when the initial rapture has worn off: "He is not the fulfillment of all I need after all." Such a one must develop other interests and other human relationships, along with a deep relationship with God. No one human person can be anyone's total fulfillment.

If I seek all my needs in my friend and expect him to be absolutely everything for me, sooner or later he will recoil from me. For I demand too much of him, perhaps not in obvious ways, but by subtly making him more and more the one in whom I seek fulfillment in every way. Depending excessively on him for my happiness, I begin to cut myself off from other influences and outlets and to place the whole burden of my happiness on him. I am asking him to do the impossible. I am imposing on him more than he can bear. I am making a god of him, expecting what no human friend can give and what I have no right to expect.

Because I require too much of him, he is bound to resent my demands. His love for me is being asked to do something that it cannot do and should not try to do. Even though he loves me, he begins to withdraw from me in his resentment of my excessive demands. I do nothing without him and go nowhere without him, like the wife, for example, who has no interests outside her husband; and my unreasonable dependence upon him becomes an intolerable burden for him.

Because I am so wrapped up in him, I have no interest in other projects or in other people, and I cut myself off from potential friends. Thus, I impoverish both myself and my friend, for through my lack of involvement with other people, I become less a person and have less to bring to his happiness and mine.

When I sense his resentment of the burden I have placed on him and see that he is beginning to withdraw, I am deeply pained and think that he no longer loves me. And I am pained that my needs, or rather my demands, are not being satisfied.

My friend is pained by his unwillingness to hurt me. Perhaps he will continue to try to be everything for me, thinking that faithful love has to bear such a burden. But all the while that he tries to be faithful to my wishes, he continues to suffer resentment.

He is taking the wrong course of action if he continues to try to be everything for me. True love not only does not have to bear this unreasonable burden, but is actually hurting the loved one in trying to do so. To keep the one I love in excessive dependence upon me is not life-producing but death-dealing. Real love makes the other party grow.

One of the signs of growth is the expansion of the person's field of interest and involvement. If he narrows his attention to one friend alone, his personality will contract. We see this in the pathetic case of the wife whose husband lets her depend upon him like a child. Her development has been retarded; she is no person at all. By continuing to try to be everything for her, he lets her die; for he is not God, he cannot be everything for her.

This is clear from the analogy of the child who is allowed to cling too closely to his mother's apron strings. At some stages of life it is good and healthy to be dependent. At two or three or four years, dependence is life-giving. But at eight or nine or ten, if the child is still at home with his mother, without playmates, without constructive interests, he will not develop as a person. The mother must make him go out from her exclusive influence even though this will hurt. But it will not be injurious, it will be life-producing.

So, too, a friend who feels the burden of his friend's excessive dependence upon him must have the courage to talk it out with the friend. The temptation is to withdraw from the relationship completely. But faithfulness requires that he continue in it. In love, he must be willing to hurt the friend temporarily by breaking the excessive dependence and calling him or her to new richness through the development of other interests and relationships.

By its very nature, we have seen, true friendship helps the friends grow by enabling them to go out to others. When one has acquired security and self-esteem in being loved, he is able to love many others also. When that point is reached, a friend must go out to others; otherwise he stops growing. He stops growing because he has mistakenly fastened his whole interest in the one friend.

But thereby he jeopardizes the very existence of the friendship. For the sake of the friendship itself, each of the friends must broaden his interests and enrich his life and personality. Otherwise the other will tend to lose interest in him.

For friends are drawn together in the first place by the mystery and richness they find in one another. We are thirsty for the fullness of being; we realize that we are very limited and not complete in ourselves. We hunger to be more than we can be by ourselves. So we are attracted to another who seems to have something to offer to our being. We are drawn by the mystery of the other person, by the other's fullness which somehow fills up what is wanting to us.

If such attraction and relationship are to continue and deepen, we have to be able to find something ever new in the other person, something which will enhance our own being. But if the other person stops growing, then his friend will lose interest in him. There is nothing new to discover in him, nothing exciting or thrilling. He expects his friend to give everything while he himself has nothing new to offer.

The very condition for maintaining a friendship is the continuing growth and development of each of the friends. For the sake of the continuing friendship, then, a friend must spur his friend on to become involved in other persons and projects. Only the continuing growth thus resulting in the friend will preserve the initial reason for the friendship, the richness and mystery of the person which make him attractive and interesting and enriching.

If friends are drawn together in the first place by awe over the mystery of the other's wonderful being, the greatest joy of friendship consists in the continuing wonderment and awe in the ever-increasing richness and beauty of the loved one. But I myself am inadequate to bring about all this development in my friend. Therefore, my love and appreciation of him encourage him to develop a variety of other relationships, for one's fullest development can be achieved only within a network of relationships within the total human community and, above all, within a deep relationship with the Lord.

I should never minimize the pain my friend will endure when I refuse to let him be excessively centered upon me. His letting go of too tight a grasp on me will not be easy for him, and I must be patient with him—but not forever! The more quickly he gets involved in other interests, the easier it will be for him to bear the pain of breaking his excessive dependence on me. He will complain that my very attempt to set him free from too great a preoccupation with me has destroyed the value for him of everything else, for he wanted to share all else with me. However, he must recover the real value of all other involvements precisely by experiencing their intrinsic value through real involvement in them.

Every pain in friendship is related to a call to the lordship of the Lord God. Anything that we grasp too tightly, whether it be a friend, or our possessions, or our accomplishments, is an obstacle to full possession by the Lord. Only faith in the Lord makes it possible to let go of other things in which we find our security and fulfillment in a false way. I am doing my friend a favor in refusing to be his or her lord, for only the Lord God can fulfill my friend's ultimate need for friendship. Then, in the Lord, I will find my friend anew, and my friend will find me anew, in a more wonderful way.

FIVE

LOVING APPRECIATION IN ADULT FRIENDSHIPS

In a loving family, a child becomes sensitized to love and learns to respond with love. The experience of loving appreciation in the home gives him some measure of self-esteem, frees him from excessive preoccupation with self, and thus makes it easier for him to love both God and fellowman. Family love opens him directly to God's own love which is imaged to him in the family and enables him to go out more and more to his fellowmen in love.

But it is not enough for a person to be loved and appreciated only in his childhood days. For full growth in love both for God and for neighbor, a person needs to be loved and appreciated not simply as a child by parents and elders, but as an adult by other adults. He needs to be loved and appreciated as an adult so that he can blossom and bear fruit in the maturity of adult love, the love which is total giving, in contrast with a child's love for his parents, which is almost total receiving. For full maturity, one needs to be loved not simply in a parent-child relationship, but in an intimate friend-to-friend relationship.

For full maturity in the life in the Spirit, one needs to be loved in friendships with people who live fully in the Spirit.

Adult friendships are necessary for the maturing of our intimate friendship with God. A child's relationship with God, and any immature person's relationship with God, has many of the characteristics of a child's dependence upon his parents. All that is good as far as it goes, but it is not enough for an adult relationship with God. Before we can relate to God on the level of close friend and not simply immature child of God, we have to learn to relate to our fellowmen on the level of friendship with our peers.

Sometimes even priests and religious have been childish, like little boys or girls, in their relationship with God, because they are still like little boys or girls in their relationships with adults. They have had no experience of close friendships with other adults who are their peers. And only too often their superiors have treated them like children.

Therefore, no matter how loving were the appreciation and esteem they received from parents and teachers in their childhood home and school, they need adult friendships if they are to mature in their friendship with God. Their adult friends must be the image of God to them in a different way than their parents were.

The intimacy of adult friendship in the Spirit can teach us to aspire to the fullest possible intimacy with the Lord himself. The tenderness of one friend toward another is the image of God's own tenderness, when the friends truly love each other in the Spirit.

HUMILITY AND SIMPLICITY: FRUIT OF LOVING APPRECIATION

The loving appreciation we receive from a friend can actually help us toward the gospel qualities of childlike simplicity and openness to God, which are not the childishness we spoke of above, but a high form of Christian maturity. To say that I must grow out of my little-boy relationship with God is not to say that I have to grow out of the attitude of "little child" in the gospel sense, which represents a truly adult relationship with God. I must pass from childish to childlike, from immaturity to the maturity of complete simplicity of heart, the simplicity which no longer needs the duplicity of pretending to be lovable. Simplicity is the attitude of one who is truly loved. Duplicity, pretense, and deceit are characteristics of the unloved, who are desperately trying to win love and attention by putting on a front of false worth.

If our friends love us truly in the Lord, it is comparatively easy for us to remain humble and unsophisticated, childlike in the gospel sense. For we can forget self, and no longer need to assert self in false pretense in order to win attention, only when we are sincerely loved and appreciated for our true worth, and this worth develops and becomes a reality in the sun of this appreciation. This worth or loveableness consists above all in our loving generously in response to love.

Attention won by pride and pretense is such a poor substitute for loving appreciation! If friends love us truly, it is comparatively easy for us to remain humble and un-sophisticated, childlike in the gospel way, free of the insecurity of doubting our lovableness, surrendered to God in absolute faith in his intimate love for us, the love which alone can make us fully lovable.

Once again, we see the importance of the apostolate of friendship. When we have experienced a friendship in the Spirit, in which the friend's love for us is nothing but total giving and joyous encouragement and appreciation of our worth, we come to a fuller appreciation of the Lord's own generous love for us, imaged to us in the friend's love. This can only result in our total freedom to give unstintingly, joyously, wholeheartedly to all others.

True friendship in the Lord opens us in love to everyone. It opens us to the experience of God. It keeps us humble and unassuming, saving us from the need to build up walls of defensiveness, which subconsciously are intended to protect us from being hurt by our fellowmen but which at the same time are walls between us and God. For the unloved one cannot believe that anyone, even God, can love him.

INTIMATE FRIENDSHIPS OF THE SAINTS

Especially if we are to go on to the heights of communion with God in the full maturity of the life in the Spirit, we need to have intimate friends in the Spirit, people who themselves are approaching these same heights or who have already passed to them. Only too often persons who are far advanced in the life in the Spirit do not find adequate nourishment in the community in which they worship. The word of God as preached in the assembly or as shared among the worshipers only too often is addressed only to beginners, because the speakers themselves are but beginners.

The more advanced person, therefore, needs close spiritual friendships in which the friends can find the nourishment of the word at their own deeper level, shared with one another in spiritual conversation at this level.

Such friends, in turn, must come to the community worship to share with others what they have found, gradually lifting others to the higher level. In time, the whole community will be enriched and will have more to share with one another. Many saints had close friendships with other saints, as we saw in chapter three. We venture to say that no saint ever reached the heights without assistance from friends in the Spirit.

LETTING THE FRIEND BE HIMSELF

Friendship is not total identification of two persons who are exactly alike. Rather, it is a mutually enriching relationship of persons who retain their individuality, and who have their own specific charisms. As close and as one as they want to be to each other, they cannot live each other's lives.

This is true above all of the friendships of celibate persons, whose primary consecration is directly to the Lord and to his mission of universal love. Our friends who are celibate must be allowed total freedom to love all those whom God has given them to love and to be occupied with the Lord's work. They must also be allowed full freedom to respond directly to the Lord in the distinctive way in which he is calling them.

Because each is endowed with his or her own specific charisms, friends complement each other. This is because the mystery of Christ is infinite. The riches of Christ are inexhaustible (Col 2:3). Therefore, no one Christian can fully reflect Christ to his fellowmen. Each reflects a different aspect of the Lord's infinite riches. That is why no one can reflect Christ with any real adequacy except in communion with others.

Therefore, I allow my friend to be fully himself. Then he can bring all the more to me in our communion, making up for my own deficiencies. By the aspect of Christ which he reflects to me, my friend draws out of me some aspect of Christ which would probably have remained undeveloped in me without my friend's warm influence.

Since the feminine way of receiving and reflecting Christ differs in many ways from the masculine way, friendship between male and female is likely to be more enriching than friendship between two of the same sex. Only a woman can open a man to certain aspects of the divine mystery, just as only a man can open a woman to other aspects. No doubt this explains why many of the great saints had close friends of the opposite sex. God made the image of God male and female, and that is why practically always a religious order has its feminine as well as its masculine branches. When their religious life was truly fervent, it was because the two were mutually influencing each other for good.

SPIRITUAL CONVERSATION AND SHARED PRAYER

Friends reflect God to one another not simply by letting God shine forth in their persons to one another, but above all by reflection in that other sense: pondering together, in spiritual conversation, the wonders that God is accomplishing in their hearts, mutually revealing the secrets of their hearts to one another in loving trust.[1]

The deeper inner realities which we experience when God works in the secret of our hearts can be fully appreciated only when we reflect upon them. And reflection is at its best in exchange with another person, who witnesses to the same inner experience perhaps but has experienced different aspects of it. We tend to be one-sided and narrow-minded in our evaluation of our spiritual experiences and tend to overemphasize one facet at the expense of another.

But when I fully reverence my friend and let him be his true self, I discover quickly that he has grasped the mystery of Christ from a different point of view than I have. When he images this aspect of the Lord for me, I am drawn to integrate these new riches into my own life.

Moreover, when he is drawn to praise the Lord for the spiritual beauty he sees in me and shows me this beauty as evidence of God's love for me, I am drawn to respond more joyously and generously to God's love. By detecting and manifesting to me the image of God's love which he sees in me, he makes me more aware of God's love for me and motivates me to respond to God in greater fidelity.

Seeing my spiritual beauty with the eyes of love, he is not only drawn to imitate it but, by revealing it to me, draws forth from my heart praise and thanksgiving to God who has fashioned this in me.

Moreover, love desires to experience the Lord in the way the friend has experienced him, if this is the Lord's will. For the beauty of the Lord shines forth in the friend's experience. To the friend, running to the Lord, the friend says, "Draw me after you! Let us run together!" (Sg 1:4). We all remember how the virgin St. Lucy drew her husband to God by telling him of the angel of the Lord with which the Lord surrounded her to keep her for himself. The husband desired to see the angel, and he saw the Lord!

Nevertheless, we said friendship is never sheer identity of two persons. It is rather a rich relationship of two individuals who are different and who enrich each other by sharing these differences. My individuality must develop if I am to have something to share with my friend. Therefore, my friend must not be possessive but must allow me to be myself, else I will have nothing with which to enrich her by sharing it with her.

So that I can be myself, my friend must allow me some privacy and solitude if I am to grow. The sun withdraws its warmth and light regularly lest it kill the plant by too much of a good thing. The rain stops falling and flows away, lest it drown the plant to which it gives life. The true friend allows his partner to be alone at times, so that in quiet reflection greater experiences may germinate. That is why very small communities must guarantee to each member an inner sanctum where he or she can be alone and quiet. In larger communities it is relatively easy to find this solitude.

Privacy and solitude are absolutely necessary for even the most intimate of friendships, such as that of husband and wife. One of the blessings of consecrated celibacy is the freedom from excessive presence of loved ones, who can keep us from the solitude necessary for being fully human and alive in the Spirit. The deepest experiences of our life, and especially of prayer, cannot be communicated. They cannot even develop or exist except in silence. Only after they have germinated and grown in private can our richest human and divine qualities be somehow shared with others to enrich them.

That is why what is planted in our hearts in intimate sharing and communication must then develop in quiet separation from others. The grace of God which comes like a seed in the liturgy of the word and in the eucharistic sacrament, or in a session of shared prayer, or in spiritual conversation, produces its richest fruits only in quiet reflection and silent interior prayer. Then when it has matured in privacy, it can be shared with others all the more fully when it is brought back to prayer or conversation in common with others. Shared prayer in community is richest only when it springs forth from the quiet of interior adoration which fills the time between the prayer meetings or the liturgical assemblies.

SIX

THE RECONCILIATION OF FRIENDS

In the closeness of friendship, we have seen, we grow aware of our selfishness and sinfulness.

"If we say we have no sin," says St. John, "we deceive ourselves" (1 Jn 1:8). If we have nothing on our conscience and say we have no sin, perhaps it is because we have not really lived; we have not loved enough to become closely involved with others. That in itself could be our sin. We have been too much like hermits, shut off from our fellowmen, withdrawn from them in the fear of being hurt. Without the friction of daily human relationships, we never flame into fire, and so we think we are sinless and perfect.

But this may mean only that we are not really living because we are not really loving, and, therefore, we are not growing in the Lord. If we are not always growing, then we are already as good as dead!

In the pain of human relationships, we discover that we are sinners, ever in need of the Lord's redeeming love. Only in discovering that we are sinners do we really begin to grow in the Holy Spirit of love. Through our experience of our sinfulness, we discover that by ourselves we spoil whatever love our natural self is capable of. In conflict with our friends, we learn at last that only in Jesus and his Holy Spirit can any human beings be faithful to one another for ever.

For without Jesus and his Spirit, friends hurt one another only too often! To the extent that we are not yet living fully in the Holy Spirit, "the flesh" is certain to manifest itself. There will be misunderstandings, and we will hurt the very ones we love the most.

The greatest pain is to know that we have hurt a loved one by our blundering selfishness, our stupid sinfulness. We do not want to do that. But we do not fully realize our capacity for sin and selfishness till we have hurt someone. And it seems that we have to hurt the one we love most before we realize what sinners we really are. When we hurt those who are not close to us, too often we are unaware of what we have done. But when we love someone greatly, love's eyes quickly discern the pain of the one we have hurt, and at last we know how sinful we are (and also how great is our love for the one we have hurt) and how greatly we need the Redeemer, who alone can heal the pain we have inflicted on the other, and our own pain over that pain.

The healing in the grace of the Holy Spirit can come only in a mutual dying on the part of the friends, a dying for one another in the dying of Christ. For the death to self which is necessarily involved in the self-giving of true love and reconciliation is possible only in the gift of the Holy Spirit, given to us by the Redeemer.

If my failure in love for my friend is a sign that I am not yet living fully in the Spirit, my quick reconciliation with my friend, involving a dying to selfishness, is a sign that we are both maturing in the redeeming Christ and his love-giving Holy Spirit. The dying to self is mutual because both asking and granting forgiveness involve a death to self. Only in this way is there a resurrection of love, and a renewed and deepened loving presence to one another.

Any giving of self which involves a true death to self for love of another brings the Holy Spirit to the one who so dies to self. Love in the Holy Spirit is always love in the Redeemer. It is redeeming love; it is freeing love.

In asking forgiveness, the offending one must undergo a double death to self: a death to his self-centered pride, and a death to the specific kind of selfishness which caused the injury.

The one who forgives enters the Lord's death also, by giving self in the Lord for the sinner, the offending one. This love, receiving the friend for whom Christ died, is a new passing through Christ's death to life.

This is fully verified only when the reconciliation includes an admission of sin against the Lord as well as against the loved one. Our very coming to be reconciled with the loved one is a coming also to God our Father. The prodigal son says to his father: "Father, I have sinned against God and against you" (Lk 15:21). The return of husband to the wife he has offended, or of wife to her offended husband, or the return of a friend to an offended friend, or of brother to offended brother, is always a return also to God. "Dear, I have sinned against God and against you."

If it is not a return to God as well as to the friend, then it is not an authentic and lasting reconciliation; it is not reconciliation in the redeeming Lord and his Spirit. If it really is reconciliation in the Lord and his Spirit, then the friends' love for one another has had a resurrection in them to a deeper love than before.

All this shows how the Lord should always be our chief focus in our love for one another. Only in his redeeming love given to us in the Holy Spirit can we be forever faithful to one another. Outside his redeeming love, we are easy prey to our own selfishness, the "old self" of sinful nature, which so easily sets us against even the ones we love deeply.

Hence, St. Paul insists that all human relationships should be "in the Lord." "You children, obey your parents in everything as the acceptable way *in the Lord*" (Col 3:20). "You who are wives, be submissive to your husbands. This is your duty *in the Lord*" (Col 3:18). "Husbands, love your wives as Christ loved the church and gave himself up for her" (Eph 5:25). But this is possible only in the Lord, in the Lord's own redeeming love.

Love in the Lord is always a redeeming love. It is redeeming both for the one who loves and for the one who is loved. In his very loving in the Lord, one dies to self and is redeemed from his sinful selfishness. He frees the one he loves as well by inviting unselfish love in return. In a special way our love is redeeming when it forgives, for it brings the Lord's own forgiveness in our own, and our dying to self in forgiving is a redeeming dying with Christ.

Friends in the Lord learn to speak thus to one another: "The Lord is our bond of love, and he is faithful. If you cannot trust the faithfulness of my love, because I am a weak sinner, trust the faithfulness of the Lord's love which keeps me—and you! Our Lord is so faithful to us that he makes us be faithful to him and to one another despite ourselves. Our fidelity to one another is the Lord's fidelity to us."

This is true in two ways. First, his faithful love for us gives us the grace of faithful love for one another. Secondly, his faithful love for us is given to us *in* our faithful love for one another. Each of us is truly, for the other, the image of God's love: presence and manifestation of God's love.

If our fidelity to one another is the Lord's fidelity to us, our fidelity to one another is also our fidelity to the Lord. In sinning against our friend, we sin against the Lord. In loving one another truly, we love the Lord himself.

Only when we begin to be unfaithful to the Lord can we begin to doubt each other's faithful caring. The moment we go out of the Lord in selfishness, we begin to doubt the other's love for us, because in our selfishness, we expect from him what he has no right to give, or what we have no right to expect.

If our friend offends us, in total trust in the Lord, in full readiness to forgive, we patiently await the prodigal one's return.

"Only when I stop speaking to you about the Lord should you doubt my love for you, because you are his marvelous best gift to me!"

PART TWO

SEVEN

FROM FRIENDSHIP TO INTIMACY WITH GOD

The purpose of friendship, we said, is to help one another grow to the fullest. God has made us in such a way that we can grow from within only under the influence of others, only if called forth by someone's love for us, like a plant which grows only under the influence of the sun.

In a special way, Christian friendship is meant to help us grow in our relationship with the Lord, as one intimately loved by him. It is meant to give us some small experience of what it means to be at home in communion with the Holy Trinity. Only in intimacy with the Lord are we the deepest "who we are." Only in communion with him are we our truest selves.

The usual way God makes us grow in our relationship with him is through the love in Christian friendship. All spiritual growth is loving response to God's love, and so the essence of growth in the Lord is knowing and believing how intimately we are loved by God, and responding in love. But usually we cannot believe God loves us in an intimate way unless we have experienced the reality of intimacy in a human way.[2]

Our deepest selves are made for a participation in the Trinity. But that is why we are made for human friendship also. Intimacy with God can be reached best in intimacy with our fellowmen, and human friendship in the Lord is meant to lead us to intimacy with God. The scriptures teach emphatically that there is no love of God without love of neighbor. Jesus makes it clear that we can be his friends only by being friends of one another. "I have called you friends. You are my friends if you do what I command you. This is my commandment, that you love one another as I have loved you" (Jn 15:15, 14, 12).

Though human friendship is meant to lead us to intimacy with God, this friendship is no mere means to this intimacy. It is never a mere scaffolding which falls away once we are closely united with God. It is a participation in the very friendship which unites the three divine Persons, and therefore it remains forever.

INTIMACY WITH GOD

Friendship, we said, frees me from the preoccupation with self in which I am incessantly wondering whether I am lovable. In this freedom from self-centeredness I am open to the touch of God.

There are people who, even in prayer, are so preoccupied with self that they cannot possibly be free to experience the more intimate interior touches of God's presence. It is useless to speak of interior prayer to them. They will not be able to pray in any real way until they have been freed from self-preoccupation. As we have seen, loving friendship is perhaps the best way to this freedom.

Some people are so wrapped up in self in their prayer that they get angry with God when he does not grant them what they ask. Theirs is a God to whom they address demands, because they do not really trust in his love for them. Obviously they have had no deep experience of his love. Perhaps this is because they are so enslaved by their doubts about their lovableness that they cannot surrender to his love; they cannot be open to the intimate touch of his loving presence. The freeing experience of human love in the Lord would help them open themselves in surrender to God's love.

The deepest mystery of revelation is that God loves each one of us intimately, with so intimate a love! But the word intimate describes an experience of God, a reality that is mysterious and deep. If I have never had an experience of what intimacy is, if I have never been known and loved in a human way, how can I know what it means that God wants to love me with an intimate love?

The experience of being known and loved in a special way in human friendship frees me from disbelief, opens me to believe that God could love me in a special way. If no human being—and a human being is infinitely less than God—has paid any attention to me or cherished me, can I believe that God, the infinite maker of the universe, is going to pay intimate attention to me? If I have never known human love and intimacy, how can I be interested if I am told that the three divine Persons want to love me and make their home in me? The doctrine of the intimate indwelling of the three divine Persons in my heart is meaningless to me if I have never experienced intimacy of any kind.

There are people who claim, of course, that even though they have no close human friends, they have intimately experienced God. We grant that God can give the experience of himself to anyone he pleases and in any way he sees fit. But here we are speaking of his more usual way of working. Even in these unusual cases, friendship would be of great benefit in bringing to deeper fulfillment what God has begun in the secrecy of those hearts.

Christian friendship, giving me the experience of being at home in intimacy, prepares me to be more fully at home with the Holy Trinity, the three divine Persons who desire to give us their intimate love and to make their home in us.

Christian friendship not only frees me for intimacy with the Lord; it actually impels me toward that intimacy. For it reveals to me that ultimately only the Lord can fulfill my deepest need for intimacy. It is only in the Trinity that we are completely at home.

The more I experience human intimacy, the more I become aware of its limitations. More and more I realize its inability to satisfy totally the infinite capacity of my heart. Therefore, experiencing the limitations of human intimacy, I long more and more for intimacy with God, whether or not I realize I am longing for him.

Human intimacy is always limited, because I can neither be fully known by another human being, nor can I be fully united in perfect communion with another human being. Even married people experience this, and that is why St. Paul suggests that they may want to abstain from sexual intimacy at times to give themselves to prayer (1 Cor 7:5). The very intimacy they have experienced with each other makes them hunger for intimacy with God. The very bodies, through which they express their communion in spirit with each other, are seen sometimes to get in the way of the total mutual interpenetration which they desire.

The very need for bodies to express their deepest communion with each other shows that this communion itself is limited by their inability totally to merge spiritually with each other. Thus, their bodies are needed to express the communion of their persons, yet those bodies somehow are in the way of their total merging into each other. God alone can penetrate other persons through and through by his loving presence.

Much as I long totally to be known by one who loves me, I cannot fully reveal myself to another human being in the way that I am known by God, because I do not even know myself fully. There are depths of my being which no other human being can penetrate or know. Only God can know me through and through, and only he, by his presence in me, can make me so thoroughly lovable that I no longer fear total transparency.

There are areas of myself which cannot be communicated to a human being in any way, areas which can be given only to God and given to him only when he takes possession of them by giving himself totally to me, coming to me, penetrating my deepest substance with his own substance, filling me with himself, possessing me totally, loving me entirely, rejoicing in me lovingly, delighting in my love for him given in response to his love for me. In my love for him I can only surrender to his transforming love, becoming entirely his in the rapturous communion of divine friendship.

My profound desire to be known in the fullest intimacy possible, to be fully revealed to loving appreciation, can be fulfilled only by God's loving knowledge of me.

Only he penetrates the depths of my being, not simply by his scrutiny and loving approval of what he sees, but by his very presence in me, making me worthy of this love. It is his loving presence in me and his self-communication to me which make me truly lovable, lovable as his own child in whom he takes delight as in the Beloved Son, lovable as his servant whom he calls friend, lovable as his spouse whom he unites to himself in transforming union. The Father delights in me as his son or daughter, his Son my Lord delights in me as his servant and friend, the Holy Spirit delights in me as his bride.

Human friendship in the Lord will always carry with it the experience of a wonderful fullness, but also the experience of its limitations, the experience of separation, of a certain degree of frustration, of almost a suffering of not being able to be as one with the friend as I would like to be. Thus, the deeper my human friendship, the more I will experience the longing for the Trinity. For in the fullness of Christian friendship, I will have some taste of the fullness which is possible but at the same time an experience of what is not possible in human friendship. Thus, whether I know it or not, I will ache for the Holy Trinity. The very experience of limitation in human friendship is an impulse toward the Blessed Trinity, who alone can give me the fullness of intimacy for which I was created. The pain of separation from a human friend becomes sign and symbol of the pain of separation from and longing for the Holy Trinity. It is only in the Lord that I can be completely at home, for he alone can know and appreciate me down to the deepest depths of my being.

It is only at prayer, in the deepest forms of interior prayer, that I can fully experience complete at-homeness with the three divine Persons. That cannot really be experienced fully at the same time that I am focused upon someone else. The deepest form of at-homeness has to be between me and the Lord. Even at liturgical prayer, there is something between me and God going on deeply inside me that cannot be shared with anybody because it is so intimate.

Christian friendship, then, gives us some taste of what it means to be "at home"—totally known, completely accepted and loved and free. But ultimately, only with the Lord can we really experience what it is to be finally at home. Only the Lord fully satisfies my God-given need for intimacy. He is the one who really loves intimately, in a way which is not possible to mere creatures, for he alone can penetrate my deepest substance, uniting the very substance of his own being with mine, thus making it possible for me to know him even as I am known by him. "Now we see indistinctly, as in a mirror; then we shall see face to face. My knowledge is imperfect now; then I shall know even as I am known" (1 Cor 13:12; see also Galatians 4:9).

EIGHT

FRIENDSHIP: SYMBOL OF GOD'S INTIMATE LOVE

Is it true that we cannot experience God's intimacy until we have experienced the intimacy of human love?

It would seem that human intimacy is in no way necessary for the experience of divine intimacy, for I can experience God's intimacy only when he directly unites himself to me, working in my heart without the intermediary of any creature. For God cannot be expressed adequately in anything created.

Divine intimacy is a direct experience of God. It is the direct effect of the very presence of God's Spirit in my heart; it is the immediate touch of the Word, God's Son; it is the Father himself holding me in his bosom. That is why a person who has no deep human friendships can still claim that he or she has had some experience of intimacy with God.

And yet it is true that through the mediation of human intimacy God brings us to the full appreciation of divine intimacy. For what God is doing directly in our hearts very often eludes our awareness. His touch is sometimes so delicate, so tender, that we scarcely notice it. Because of this lack of awareness, we fail to respond fully to his presence in our hearts. Consequently, we do not get its full benefit.

It is of the greatest importance that we cultivate the awareness of his intimate touch. Our most powerful motivation for faithful, wholehearted love for God is appreciative awareness of his tender love for us. If we are to experience God's intimate touch, we must cultivate stillness, silence, and solitude, because the Lord's touch is often soft and tender like a gentle breeze. A light breeze cannot be perceived by a person who is incessantly moving about in activity.

But silence and interior prayer are not the only way to awareness of God's tender love for us. We have noted how preoccupation with self prevents us from awareness of the interior touch of God. The experience of human friendship in the Lord can bring us to a fuller awareness of God's workings in our heart in at least two ways:

First, human friendship makes us tender and more sensitive to others, and therefore to God. It opens us, brings us out of ourselves, frees us from self-preoccupation so that we are more alert and responsive to others and to the Lord. It enables us to forget self in concern for others.

Secondly, human love in the Lord is a symbol or sacrament of God's love. By symbol we do not mean a sign which is completely separate from the reality it stands for, in the way that an engagement ring is something different from the promise it signifies. By symbol we mean a sign which is an embodiment and expression of the very reality it symbolizes, because it is a sharing in that reality. The truly Christian love of husband and wife, for example, symbolizes the reality of Christ's love for his Church not simply because it is in the likeness of that love, but because it is a real participation in Christ's love for his people. Therefore, the husband and wife's love for each other in the Lord is an expression and manifestation of Christ's love for his Church and for each of these two. Christ expresses his love through this man and this woman's love for each other in the Spirit.

Thus, human love in the Lord is a concrete tangible expression of God's own love, for God's love has been poured out into our hearts by the Holy Spirit who has been given to us (Rom 5:5). Thus, my friend's love for me in the Holy Spirit is one with God's love for me, to the extent that it springs simultaneously from my friend's heart and from the Holy Spirit who dwells in that heart.

In this way, friendship in the Lord is God's own love embodied and made present to one another in the friends' love for each other. That is why friendship can make us aware of God's personal love for us; it can lead us to believe firmly that God wills to give us an even deeper, more direct experience of his intimacy.

But even though God's love for me is symbolized and manifest to me in my friend's love for me, the reality symbolized, that is, God's intimate personal love for me, works its most wonderful effects directly in my heart, without human mediation. Just as God's word, spoken to me by a preacher of the word, achieves its saving effect in me only if, through the mediation of the word, God works simultaneously in the interior of my heart by the inner "word" of his grace, so, too, human love mediates God's love to me only if at the same time God's love is working directly in my heart. His preached word is symbol and pledge of the more profound and continued working of the inner word of grace in my heart. In the same way, the human love which mediates and symbolizes God's love to me is symbol and pledge of a still more intimate and direct working of his love in the secret of my heart.

Thus, the experience of human love in the Lord can help make us more fully aware of the wonders which God is already working secretly in our hearts by the presence of his Holy Spirit but which we have not yet adequately appreciated. God's workings in our heart are so profound and divine that they surpass all human understanding and, therefore, go easily unnoticed and unresponded to. Human tenderness in the Lord can bring us to an appreciation of God's tenderness toward us, which perhaps we have taken too much for granted and have not appreciated. It can make us desire to be more with the Lord in stillness, so that we can become more and more aware of what he is doing in the secret of our heart by his loving presence.

THE SYMBOL IS NOT THE FULL REALITY

Although the experience of human love can sensitize us to God's tender love, God's deepest intimacy, we said, is given and experienced only in direct union with his Word and Spirit dwelling in the deepest depths of our heart. His spiritual touch is fully given and fully appreciated only in our deepest interior.

This is not to say that his interior spiritual touch is never accompanied by, embodied in, or mediated through the touch of human love. In intimate communion with a human friend, one often does have an authentic experience of communion with God, who manifests himself in the midst of this love. For unselfish love in the Lord is a participation in God's own love and a symbol of it. And yet, as a symbol, it is only a participation in God's love, not the divine fullness of that love. A symbol is not the fullness of the reality it symbolizes.

Though it is a real participation in the reality and a manifestation of it, the total reality is immeasurably greater than the symbol. Christ's communion with his Church, for example, obviously overflows infinitely beyond the communion of a man with his wife which symbolizes it. So, too, the love in the Spirit uniting Christ and his Church is symbolized and expressed by the love in a religious community, but the total reality of the love uniting Christ and his Church cannot be contained in the one community.

As symbol of the more wonderful interior reality of divine intimacy, human intimacy points to the deeper reality and invites us to it. Therefore, even though we rejoice in and appreciate the human touch which can convey the divine touch, we would be wrong to stop with the human touch and rest in it as though it were the ultimate experience of God's tenderness. We must not forget that it is only an invitation to something more divine, which can be granted to us only when our hearts are totally focused on the Lord alone in the solitude of profound interior prayer.

We can never say, then, that our full communion with God is experienced in our communion with one another. Bonhoeffer appreciated this fact and said that to long for the transcendent when you are in your wife's arms shows, to put it mildly, a lack of taste. Just as the fullness of prayer would distract a man from his wife, so the fullness of attention to his wife distracts him from the fullness of intimacy with God.

Not only Bonhoeffer, but all Christian tradition, as far back as St. Paul, realized this (1 Cor 7:32–35). The ancient preface for the consecration of virgins, composed in the fifth century by St. Leo the Great, states that a Christian marriage is a symbol of the union of Christ and his bride the Church. But the consecrated virgin bypasses the symbol and strives to live the full reality of direct union with Christ. What marriage points to, the virgin strives to live directly. The consecrated virgin is herself a sign that marriage is a symbol, not the fullness of the reality.

Her life without a husband is a perpetual sign to the married that they must beware of getting so lost in the symbol that they miss the deeper reality. We might point out here the danger of confusing a lesser experience with the experience of God. An esthetic experience, for example, is not necessarily of itself an experience of God, though it is sometimes taken to be such. A young man may claim, for example, that listening to symphonic music is all the experience of God that he needs, and that liturgical worship is superfluous. Or a person may spurn the inspired word of God in the psalms, saying that he finds God in the beauty of the sunset, and that this is enough for him. There is no doubt that an esthetic experience can wonderfully sensitize us to the experience of God, and that God can and sometimes does communicate the experience of himself in the midst of an esthetic experience or in the power of the storm. But the two do not necessarily go together, and a profound esthetic experience is possible without any true experience of God at all.

Moreover, it would be wrong to rest in the esthetic experience as though it were the ultimate experience. Like the experience of human intimacy, it points to a more profound interior experience of God which can be granted only in the profound silence and solitude of the heart.

I know a man who always experiences sadness in the midst of an esthetic experience, because the glory of a brilliant sunset or the beauty of a musical composition is only such a faint reflection of the glory of God that it only makes him long for God himself. In the midst of these other experiences he longs for God himself in direct union. Indeed, sometimes in the midst of the beauty of nature or of song, one is distracted by it from the interior touch of God's presence in the heart, and one has to turn aside from the music or from the natural beauty to give full attention directly to the Lord and to experience the touch of his own indwelling presence in the heart.

So, too, the ecstasy of human love, like the esthetic experience, does not necessarily bring with it an experience of God, and even if sometimes it does, it is only a symbol pointing to something greater to which God is calling us. The lesser experiences, however, certainly can help sensitize us to the greater experiences, and one persistent theme in this book is that human love in the Spirit makes us more open to the direct touch of the Spirit in our hearts.

In addition to the intimacy of human friendship in the Lord, then, the Christian must spend time in direct adoration of the Lord himself. Only in silent adoration can the fullness of divine intimacy be experienced. Were friends to rest in their intimacy with one another as though this were the ultimate experience, were they greedily to hold on to this experience, keeping one another from the experience of deeper intimacy with God in prayer and adoration, they would be guilty of sloth.

Sloth is so resting in the enjoyment of God's lesser gifts that one neglects or rejects his more divine gifts. It is holding on to the lesser gifts so tightly that one is not open to receive the greater gifts. It is unwillingness to die to some of the lesser joys given by God in order to come alive to the greater ones he still has in store. It is a refusal to grow. It is a resting in the lesser experience as though it were the ultimate.

In human relationships, sloth is the failure to bring our friend to the better things, because we rest in the pleasure of possessing him, holding on to him, holding him back when we should be urging him on to greater things. Friends in the Lord say to one another, "Come, let us run to the Lord!" (Sg 1:4).

NINE

FRIENDSHIP IN THE SPIRIT

Friendship in the Spirit is the greatest of the works of the Lord, because it is the perfection of God's image in mankind. As image or symbol of divine friendship, Christian friendship is already a taste or experience of the divine friendship which exists among the three Persons of the Trinity. Therefore, it makes us hunger ever more for the fullness of the divine friendship. The symbol points to the deeper reality and invites us more and more into it.

Even though friends do not rest in the symbol, but encourage and help one another to the reality of direct intimacy with God, they do not abandon the symbol as though it were only a temporary means to God; they remain close friends forever. In silence and adoration they deepen their intimacy with God but then turn to one another again to express and symbolize their divine intimacy in their human friendship. The more they enter into the full reality of direct communion with God, the richer is the human friendship, the symbol in which they express their friendship with God.

FRIENDSHIP IS FOREVER

For the symbol is an expression of God's own love, operative in their love for one another, and therefore it continues even in eternity. Love remains forever, though the charisms pass away (1 Cor 13:13). As the friends grow in closeness with God and with one another, their friendship as symbol expresses ever more fully and perfectly the reality of God's own love working in the hearts of men.

Of itself, their friendship opens the friends to love others, too, not just one another. Friendship with God has this effect even more. The more our friendship is rooted in the Lord and expresses friendship with him, the broader our hearts are in loving a multitude of others. But if love for a friend gives us power to love others, then certainly it increases our power to love the friend himself.

Thus, friendship is meant to last forever. It is not a stage that falls away when we have used it to come to divine intimacy and to universal love of our fellowmen. It is not a mere means to God which is to be cast aside when it has served its purpose. For I do not love others only as a means to friendship with the Holy Trinity. A person is never a means to an end. He is always an end in himself, to be loved for his own sake. I love him with God's own love, as image of God, as God's own son, as magnificent creation of God's love, wonderfully lovable in himself, forever to be loved.

But since a person is completed and fully himself only in loving relationships with others, so, too, the love and friendship which unite persons and bring them to fulfillment are never a means but always an end. Friendship is the fullness and completion of persons. It is not something added to people to join them together, and it is not just their mutual love. It is their very lives brought to perfection by being joined in love and lived together as one.

Thus, human friendship is never just a means to be used; it is an end to be enjoyed for its own sake. As an end in itself, of course, it is subordinate to the ultimate end. It is part of the fullness of the ultimate end, which is our communion with God in communion with all his friends.

FRIENDSHIP: IMAGE AND GLORY OF GOD

Thus the image of God, three Persons in one life, is perfected in human persons only to the extent that they are friends, since they are fully persons only in the relationship of love and friendship, sharing with one another their life in the Spirit. That is why friendship in the Lord, as the fullness of mutual knowledge and love, is the fullness of the image and likeness of God. Since friends in the Lord are one in the Word of divine knowledge and in the Holy Spirit of love, their friendship is a participation in the friendship of the three divine Persons and is an expression of that friendship. This beautiful expression of the Holy Trinity in the friends' love for one another is a manifestation and glorification of the Trinity. Friendship in the Lord is thus "the image and glory of God" (1 Cor 11:7).

The words "image" and "glory" are practically synonyms. Each denotes a presence and manifestation of God. But "glory," even more than "image," connotes a manifestation of God in power and splendor. Christian love powerfully draws others to the love of God. Friendship in the Lord is a sharing in the life and Spirit which the friends have from God. The Lord's life in us, rooted and grounded in his personal presence in the deepest heart of each, is fully expressed only in the loving communion of all who are in the Lord (Eph 4:14–17).

The full dimensions of love in the Spirit can be experienced only in the fullness of Christian community. The closer we are to Jesus as our personal Lord, the closer we are to all who are in the Lord. But our intimacy with all God's people is expressed and manifest in our friendship with those friends who are closest to us in the Lord. The beauty and joy of authentic Christian friendship are a witness to the beauty and joy of God and draw others into this love and joy.

Because friendship in the Spirit, a magnificent work of the Lord, thus glorifies the Holy Trinity, friends in the Lord do not disappear from one another's lives to be replaced solely by the Lord. Rather, their friendship manifests the presence of the Lord and his Spirit of love. They "decrease" by dying to selfishness, only to be filled with the Lord and his love in the Spirit. The Lord "increases" as I and my friend decrease, because his love more and more fills our love, not destroying it, but transforming it into his own divine love. Our love as friends is totally transformed in his love, becoming but one love with his.

That is why friends in the Lord—and this is certainly true of husband and wife—can actually aspire to receive together the transforming union with God. Their union with one another will thus be transformed in union in God. And so it will be eternal union with one another in God. Even death will not be able to separate them from one another. God will be glorified in their love for one another, their loving appreciation of and joy in each other.

THE WITNESS OF ST. CATHERINE

Such is the teaching of St. Catherine of Siena, Doctor of the Church. Thinking no doubt of her intimate circle of friends, and especially of Bl. Raymond, Catherine tells us in her *Dialogue* that friendship remains forever. In the following words she is describing the life of glory in heaven. God is speaking:

> In love, the blessed rejoice in the eternal vision of me, sharing together in the infinite good which is myself. This is because on earth they have lived in love of me and of one another. Besides enjoying me together, they rejoice and exult in one another, sharing in each other's good with love's affection.
>
> And they have a special sharing with those whom they closely loved with particular affection in the world. For in this affection for one another, they grew in grace and increased in virtue. Each was the occasion of manifesting to the other the glory and praise

> of my name, in themselves and in their neighbor. In the eternal life they have not lost their love for one another, but have it still, sharing intimately with one another more abundantly than before. Their mutual love is added to the universal good in which they share with all. . . .
>
> When a person arrives at eternal life . . . he rejoices in me and in the other persons who are with him, and in the blessed spirits. For in these others he sees the beauty and tastes the sweetness of my love.[1]

Not only in eternity, but even now on earth, friendship in the Lord reveals the beauty and sweetness of God's love. Friends glorify God by their love for one another, when they appreciate and rejoice in one another precisely as a wonderful work of the Lord. Friendship in the Lord is the greatest of the works of the Lord, for it is the perfection of God's image and glory in man. It is a participation in and manifestation of the life and love of the three divine Persons, and therefore it is a glorification of the Holy Trinity.

It manifests and glorifies God more wonderfully than all else in creation. It is the fullness of the Son of God himself, in whom God is glorified, for each friendship in the Lord is an integral part of the great network of covenant love in which all things are brought together in unity in Christ and his love.

A PSYCHOLOGIST'S TESTIMONY

The psychologist Maslow describes mature human love as primarily appreciative love, a love filled with wonderment and awe at the perfections of the loved one. He distinguishes two kinds of love: the deficiency love of the immature person, and the being love of the mature person—D love and B love.[2]

The average individual is motivated by deficiencies. He is seeking to fulfill his basic needs for security, for self-esteem and respect, for belonging and love. He is capable of "D love," deficiency love, need love, selfish love. He perceives the loved one as a useful object, a means to satisfy his deficiency. Hence, he is demanding and self-centered in his love. He shapes others in an exploiting and purposeful way.

But the healthy mature person, because his needs have been cared for, is motivated primarily by the higher need to develop his full potential in giving to others, in creative outgoing forces which give deepened life to others. He is capable of "B love"—love for the being of a person, love unselfish and unending.

The B lover perceives the loved one as an end experience, loving him for his own sake. He is fascinated by and has respect for the intrinsic nature of the loved one. As a result, the B lover has a spontaneous admiration, undemanding wonder, and awe for the loved one. He creates the loved one, giving him a self-image, self-acceptance, and self-esteem, all of which make him grow.

In mature friendship in the Lord, the friends are filled with wonderment at the other's beauty precisely as a work of the Lord. When the friends are focused upon one another in this spontaneous admiration of the wonders which God has accomplished in them, then the Lord is fully Lord in their relationship. They do not lord it over each other, making self the focus of attention and demand.

In their conscious affective focus on the mystery of the friend, overflowing with wonderment at the Lord's beauty revealed in the friend, the Lord is fully glorified. Because he is glorified in the friends' appreciation of each other, their appreciation of each other intensifies their appreciation of the Lord. They have an added motivation for their praise of God in prayer, for they have tasted his sweetness and seen his beauty in the friend.

Friend does not focus incessantly on the friend, however. For we are meant above all to glorify the Lord by paying direct attention to him, focusing directly upon him. But our life is a rhythm. God has made so many exquisite wonders, and part of life's rhythm is to praise him for his glory as manifested to us in experiencing each of these wonders. The Christian is meant to glorify God in direct communion with him in deep interior prayer. But sometimes also he is to take time to enjoy the wonders of God's glory in creation, but especially his glory as manifest in his human family, who love one another in the Holy Spirit.

Thus, our total appreciation of the Lord is greatly magnified. We know God not just in the direct experience of his presence in our hearts; we know him also as revealed in his image and glory, human beings united in love.

Thus, holy persons celebrate their friendship as a value in itself. It is not just a means to God. God is glorified in this love, for in it the Holy Trinity is imaged and mirrored. Christians are not just separate persons who mirror God in their separate hearts. They are united hearts which, in their very sharing with one another what is deepest in them—their life in the Trinity—they not only mirror, but are caught up into that very mystery of exchange which is the eternal blessed Trinity.

Friends in the Lord, then, turn one another to the Lord to worship him directly. But they also praise him for one another. They cannot adequately do this unless they truly appreciate and enjoy God's life and beauty as mirrored in one another. God therefore wishes that they sometimes focus their attention on one another in loving appreciation, thus appreciating his glory as manifest in them.

Of course, then, friends should not disappear from one another's lives, but should rejoice in their friendship and enjoy it. For the image and reflection of God must not disappear, but continue forever for the glory of God.

That is why friends in the Lord, even though they rejoice above all when the friend is fully intent upon the Lord, rightly rejoice also in one another. In moments of deep sharing, they can focus on one another in a pure love which is God's love in them, God's love in which they love one another. They can celebrate their love for one another in the sheer joy of friendship as a beautiful value in itself, a value which glorifies God more than any other of his works.

But whenever friends focus on one another, to rejoice in one another as God's beautiful work, theirs must be joy in one another precisely as "God's chosen ones, holy and beloved" (Col 3:12). They must manifest toward one another all the reverence and deference which the three divine Persons have for one another. Their joy in one another is pure and beautiful to the extent that the Lord has so increased in their friendship, burning out of it all selfish usurpation of lordship, that he alone is Lord. His love alone holds sway, and the friends rejoice in one another as beloved of God, image and glory of God.

Any delight in one another is referred to the Lord in the form of praise, for we are his work. It is he who has knit us together in love in his Son. Loving appreciation of one another as God's work is itself praise, even if it is not expressed in religious song. What would be the value of religious song if we never found joy in those whom God expects us to love, and if we made no effort to nourish and cherish God's image in one another? In our very beings, knit together in love, God must be glorified!

If we rightly rejoice in all those whom we have helped by our love, then why should we not rejoice especially in our closest friends, whose love for us has helped open us to love all these others? If friends should rejoice in all those whom they have brought to God as the fruit of their love for one another, then certainly they may occasionally take time to rejoice in one another as God's precious gift.

Thus, "I must decrease" does not mean "I must disappear" from the life of my friend when my friend grows more and more in intimacy with God. Even though my love for my friend desires above all else that he or she be as completely with the Lord as possible, this does not mean that I must step out of my friend's life. On the contrary, I am more intimately with my friend than ever before, the more fully each of us is in the Lord. For the Lord is our deepest self, and he is our most intimate bond of union.

I "disappear" in the sense that I stand aside, giving my friend full freedom to be with the Lord. I "disappear" also in the sense that I give him full freedom to be fruitful in loving others, as well as me, in God's own love. But he comes back to me in joy after helping others; he comes back to me as to his home, for the closeness of friendship means being at home. But the Lord is his friend, and so more and more he takes me home with him when he turns ever more fully to his Lord. We are at home together in the Lord, with the Lord. And, together in the Lord, we are creative in loving others. Together, we are a presence of the Lord to our fellowmen. Together we praise the Lord for the wonders he has accomplished in us through our friendship with each other.

TEN

WORSHIP: THE FULLNESS OF FRIENDSHIP

Friends in the Lord always turn one another toward the Lord. They are not forever gazing at each other, but together they look to the Lord and to their brothers and sisters in the Lord.

No creature must ever be loved as an idol. John, in the Apocalypse, was so enraptured by the beauty of the angel who appeared to him, that he prostrated himself before him. "I fell at his feet to worship him but he said to me, 'No! Get up! I am merely a fellow servant with you and your brothers who give witness to Jesus. Worship God alone!'" (Rv 19:10).

Once, at a prayer meeting, someone read a passage from St. Paul about rejecting the worship of idols, about not making money, or pleasure, or power one's idol. One of the women present, after reflecting a bit on the passage, said, "When I first married my husband, I was so enraptured by love of him that I made an idol of him, not just figuratively speaking, but in reality. I worshiped him as my god. I tried to possess him so totally and exclusively for myself that I did not care whether I loved God or anyone else. And I wanted him to pay attention to me in such a way that I would be his god, just as he was mine.

"His attitude was the same as mine. We were so exclusively wrapped up in each other that there was no room for anyone else, not even God, in our lives. Love of each other was not bringing us to God. For we loved each other in the wrong way. Love does not necessarily bring the lovers to God. Love is not by itself an experience of God, as some people are claiming. Indeed, as I know by experience, it can even be used to exclude God from our lives."

The woman was speaking at a time when celibacy was being attacked viciously within the very ranks of the Catholic priesthood. Even some priests and religious sisters were making the claim that one cannot love God unless one has experienced sexual union. As the woman spoke, it was obvious to all present that she was speaking charismatically, addressing these people who thought that sexual experience is essential in coming to God. She continued her message:

"By the mercy and grace of God, my husband and I came through that selfish state, that stage of selfishness-for-two. Now we are forever pointing out the Lord to each other, and in our love for each other we are open to the love of our fellowmen as well. All that we sacrificed in dying to each other for the sake of the Lord, we now possess more wonderfully than ever in the Lord."

Any kind of friendship, we have seen, is meant to help us grow into our truest selves. Friendship in the Lord helps us to grow into who we fully are: namely, persons loved intimately by the Lord.

In friendship in the Lord, the process that takes place is a growing away from total and exclusive focus upon each other, two lovers staring forever into each other's eyes. More and more the lovers grow in the consciousness of the Lord, the one who really loves intimately.

Thus, the fullness of Christian friendship is realized only among those who let each other be fully the Lord's. They work for that with all the fullness of their being. They want nothing exclusively for themselves; they want only that their friend be fully the Lord's. The more the Lord is paid attention to and the more he is praised by the other, the more the friend rejoices. The more obviously the Lord loves the other, the more the friend rejoices. The friend's greatest joy is to see his friend totally centered on the Lord, and finds even greater joy in this than in having the friend pay attention to himself.

Friends in the Lord exercise no lordship over one another, they have no desire to be god to one another. They want the Lord alone to be fully worshiped. Thus, the fullness of friendship is worship—not worship of one another, but worship of the Lord, together. If friends die to lordship over each other, so that the Lord Jesus will be fully Lord of each and Lord of the two together, then they will recover possession of each other in a beautiful new way—in the Lord.

In the first stages of their friendship, the friends will be enthralled by the beauty they see in each other, and that is a good and normal stage. But it is not meant to end there. To try to make it end there is to set limits on what we can experience. It is to act as if this were the ultimate experience of friendship, as though there were nothing else for friends to possess and enjoy but each other.

In reality, the beauty in the other is only a taste of what God is. It should be seen as an image of God and an enticement toward him. If the two try to spend their lives trying to look at each other only, they will never be open to the absolute fullness in God of which this friend is only a taste. Gradually, the friendship is meant to become less and less two people looking at each other and more and more two people who have freed each other for God, two who look together toward God.

St. Augustine brings this out by a comparison with the two eyes in the human body. All the parts of the body are knit together in love:

> Brothers, our two eyes do not see each other; we might say they do not know each other. But in the love of the bodily frame do they not know each other?

> Do you want proof that they know each other in virtue of the love that knits them together? When both eyes are open, the right may not rest on some object on which the left shall not also rest. Try to direct the glance of the right eye without the other, if you can. Together they meet in one object, together they are directed to one object; their aim is one, their places diverse.
>
> If then all who with you love God have one aim with you, it does not matter that in the body you are separated in place; you have the eyesight of your heart fixed alike on the light of truth. (*Patrologiae Latina*, 35:2025)

This is because intimacy with the three divine Persons is the goal of us all. We are all meant to be taken into the intimacy of the divine life.

But in a real sense, this divine life is the divine Persons' mutual worship of one another. To say that the three divine Persons worship one another may sound like heresy. It is simply a striking way of expressing a profound reality of love. And love is the inner life of God. Each of the three divine Persons is totally toward the Other, in a kind of divine humility and deference to the Other. Eternally, each is enraptured by the beauty of the Other, each is rejoicing in the Other.

Father is totally focused on the Son, and Son is completely focused on the Father: "In the beginning was the Word and the Word was with God" (Jn 1:1). The Greek word translated as "with" is really a dynamic word, implying impetus toward. The Son is eternally toward the Father, intent upon him in love, praising him, glorifying him, mirroring him.

That is why, from the beginning of time, the Son as Word is forever revealing the Father, enlightening every man who comes into the world (Jn 1:9).

That is the mystery of love, and God is love. Mature human love, we have seen, is filled with wonderment and awe at the beauty of the beloved. That is the secret of the Trinity, too. The mystery of the Trinity is three Persons who have emptied themselves for one another, each glorifying the other, as it were, in self-forgetfulness.

That this is true in their inner life is indicated by their joy in pointing out each other to us. The gospel speaks of the Father's joy in revealing his Son: "Yes, Father, for such was thy gracious will!"—to reveal the mystery of your Son to "the little ones" (Lk 10:21). And of the Son's joy in revealing the Father: "No one knows who the Father is except the Son and anyone to whom the Son chooses to reveal him" (Lk 10:22).

Luke and Paul indicate how this revelation of the Father and Son is the work of the Holy Spirit given into our hearts by Father and Son. "Jesus thrilled with joy in the Holy Spirit" (Lk 10:21), thanking the Father for revealing his secrets to the little ones. The Spirit of the Son reveals the Father, causing us to cry out to him in desire for his loving embrace: "Abba, Father!" (Gal 4:6). The Spirit reveals both Father and Son: "He will glorify me, for he will take what is mine and declare it to you. All that the Father has is mine; therefore I said that he will take what is mine and declare it to you" (Jn 16:14–15).

Last of all the Spirit shows himself to us, for without this self-revelation, his revelation of Father and Son is incomplete.

A friend of mine who is an intimate friend of the three divine Persons and knows each of them explicitly has borne witness to this reality in a letter to me, saying, "What unbelievable life and love there must be in the Trinity, each Person desiring only that the Other be known and loved and glorified! And so the Spirit has revealed himself to me only after he has shown me the other two Persons, to whom he points, and whom he loves intimately."

What this friend of each of the three divine Persons experienced in her inner life of prayer corresponds to what the scriptures have to say on this point.

As the divine Persons want to reveal one another, so, too, friends in the Lord want to show their friends all that they themselves have seen in God. "Come and see!" said Philip to his friend Nathanael (Jn 1:46). When we have been taken into the intimacy of the divine life, we, too, like the divine Persons, are totally forgetful of self and totally intent on glorifying and praising the Other, glorifying the three divine Persons, showing them to others. Friends in the Lord, instead of becoming distractions for one another, free one another for deeper and deeper prayer.

If they are real friends, that is what they want for one another above all. They give the other freedom for the Lord. And they give this not as a concession, but with all their heart. That is what they want most for the other. They do not want to be the other's lord; they don't want their friend to be paying such exclusive attention to them that they cannot see the Lord. They want the other to know and praise God.

And yet, though in one way they are forgetful of each other and more intent on the Lord, in another way they uphold each other in this intentness on the Lord. Each one's own joy is deepened precisely because his friend is such a friend of the Lord. Together, and not as separate from one another, they worship the Lord. The fullness of their friendship is this worshipping together of the three divine Persons, this full participation in the Trinity's own inner worship or joy in contemplating and loving the Other.

This is what happens in Christian liturgy, which is a beginning on earth of the eternal liturgy of heaven, in which the saints tell one another, share with one another, their own rapture in the Lord.

But is it not silly to point out to others what the others are themselves already enjoying? Not at all! Our own joy is all the deeper the more we are aware that others are enjoying with us the things which give us such delight. I once attended a seminar in the French Alps at a monastery on a ridge directly opposite Mont Blanc. Instead of coffee breaks between our sessions, we were more wonderfully refreshed simply by going outdoors and gazing at the glorious white peak surrounded by the glory of the lesser peaks. But we never enjoyed this beauty in silence, because one delightful, delighted French Dominican kept grabbing our arms and pointing to the majestic peak, "Voila! Mont Blanc!" He just couldn't keep still. He could enjoy it fully only in showing it to us, only in being sure that the rest of us were enjoying it too.

So it is with friends in the Lord. Their joy in the Lord is deepened when they share him with their friends. Likewise, since each friend is a symbol and presence of God's love to the other, it is only right that God be glorified in the friend through the joyful recognition of God present in this friendship.

Friendship will reach its plenitude only in the eternal liturgy of praise and thanksgiving in heaven, when our love will rejoice in eternal gratitude to God for all the wonders he has accomplished in our friends. This liturgy is already begun in our hearts now in the form of the joy of friendship in the Lord, the joyous appreciation of what the Lord has done and is doing in the friend. We realize that this is the Lord's work, even though he has accomplished so much of it through the friendship itself, through our love for one another in the Lord.

To rejoice in our friends in heaven is to rejoice in God himself, in God as communicated to his whole people, the completed family of all his children. Just as our joy in anything is all the richer when we can enjoy it in union with those we love, so our joy in God is somehow enhanced because we enjoy him in union with all our friends.

ELEVEN

FULLNESS OF LIFE: COVENANT LOVE

"Offer to God praise as your sacrifice. . . . He that offers praise as a sacrifice glorifies me" (Ps 50:14, 23).

The most sincere sacrifice of praise we can offer to God is a life lived in all its fullness. For only by living our life to the utmost do we fully show our appreciation of God's gift of that life. Words of praise are meaningless unless they express a life lived for God's glory.

Love of life, and the joy of being human, glorifies God to the extent that it expresses reverence for life as God's gift and appreciation of his loving kindness in giving it. He gave us this life in creating each of us; he redeemed this life himself by living as man and rejoicing in his humanity, and delivering up this life for each one of us.

We best show our appreciation of life by letting it grow under the sun of God's love and doing what we can to foster this growth. We wish to give our life back to God in all its fullness so that he might have joy in us. "May the Lord rejoice in all his works! May the glory of the Lord last forever" (Ps 104:31).

"Man fully alive is the glory of God," said St. Irenaeus. But the fullness of life is covenant love: friendship with God and friendship with our brothers and sisters in Christ. Covenant love is above all loving intimacy with the three divine Persons, in joyful appreciation and acceptance of their love for us. This intimacy with God is granted to us in the new covenant in Christ's blood. In this blood we are reconciled with God and given the grace of adoption as sons in the beloved Son. We are made participants in the intimate trinitarian life of God. Only in living this life is man fully alive.

But covenant love is also love and appreciation of all who share with us in this life of the divine Persons. For only together with our brothers and sisters in Christ are we fully in the image and glory of God.

Such, then, is the sacrifice of praise, the pleasing offering to God which he accepts with joy. God is fully glorified and praised when we accept his gift of life in all its fullness, appreciating it, developing it, letting him form it in us ever more fully, expressing it fully in covenant love, and recognizing and praising the glory of God as manifest in the union of God's people in this love.

DYING TO LIVE

Fear of sufferings is simply the other side of the coin of love of life. If we love life, if we are filled with the joy of being alive and human, of course we will fear the sufferings which are a threat to this God-given love of life and the thrust toward the fullness of life.

Accepting life in its fullness, however, includes accepting the limitations and sufferings which inevitably accompany life, enduring the growing pains which are inevitable in passing from one stage of life to another.

Like the mother and her seven sons in the Book of Maccabees, we accept even sufferings from God, knowing that whatever degree of life we have, it is always a pledge of an undying fullness of life to come. In the words with which she exhorts her seven sons to give their lives bravely, in faithfulness to their covenant with God, the mother bears witness at the same time to how precious God's gift of life really is. Addressing her sons, who are being tortured to death for their faith in the God of Israel, she says:

> I do not know how you came into existence in my womb; it was not I who gave you the breath of life. nor was it I who set in order the elements of which you are composed. Therefore since it is the Creator of the universe who shapes each man's beginning, as he brings about the origin of everything, he, in his mercy, will give you back both breath and life, because you now disregard yourselves for the sake of his law. (2 Mc 7:22ff.)

There is profound reverence for human life in these words, reverence for this life from the very instant that God begins to set in order the elements of that life in the mother's womb. If a man finds himself in a situation where in witness to God he is called upon to sacrifice this life lovingly for his Creator, he offers it joyfully, in the conviction that he who gave this life in the first place will restore it in all its fullness, and even more wonderfully. In the very offering of their life in sacrifice, these seven sons drink in God's covenant love and his gift of eternal life. The last of the seven to be put to death professes this faith, saying to the tyrant, "After enduring brief pain, my brothers have drunk of never-failing life, under God's covenant" (2 Mc 7:36).

The scriptures repeatedly express wonderment and gratitude for the mystery of human life formed by God in a woman's womb. "I have gotten a man with the help of the Lord," says Eve when she conceives and bears her first son (Gn 4:1). The psalmist, too, confesses with profound awe and wonderment that the marvels which fashioned him in the womb were God's work. "It was you who created my inmost self, and knit me together in my mother's womb. For all these mysteries I thank you: for the wonder of myself, for the wonder of your works" (Ps 139:13ff.).

The words of the last of the seven sons martyred for his faithfulness to the covenant show that it was faith in God's faithfulness to his covenant which gave rise to belief in the resurrection of those who had been put to death for the covenant. "My brothers, after enduring brief pain, have drunk of never-failing life, under God's covenant." God is faithful to those who are faithful to him and will give eternal life to those who die for him.

Man's covenant love in response to God's covenant love is the fullness of the sacrifice of praise. It is the full appreciation of God's love and the gift of life bestowed by that love.

St. Paul speaks of self-sacrifice for the sake of our brothers and sisters as a pleasing sacrifice, acceptable to God. "Walk in love, as Christ loved us and gave himself up for us, a fragrant offering and sacrifice to God" (Eph 5:1). Covenant love, as *suffering* for God and for fellow men, is a sacrifice pleasing to God.

But covenant love as also *rejoicing* in the fullness of life is a sacrifice of praise to God. And this sacrifice of praise is perfect only when it overflows with the joy of fullest possible appreciation of the wonders of life and love. The fullest appreciation is expressed by living that life and covenant love in all its fullness.

The sacrifice of praise and joy, then, is life lived in all its fullness, to express appreciation of God's love. But, we said, life lived in its fullness is covenant love in its fullness; it is love joyfully giving to others all that can be given, joyfully offering even life itself in a death endured for the good of others.

We do not love sufferings as sufferings. We love only life, and we rejoice in sufferings only to the extent that they are a way to the fullness of life. "Let us keep our eyes fixed on Jesus, who inspires and perfects our faith. For the sake of the joy which lay before him, he endured the cross, heedless of its shame" (Heb 12:1).

Friends, continue to face life with all joy, living it to the full in appreciation of God's love who gave you this life. And since life is full only in love and friendship, rejoice in friendship, and thus show your appreciation of God's love which gave you this friendship. But know that even sufferings are the gift of his love, the love which is bringing you through sufferings to the fullness of life and joy. Continue above all to be apostles of joy, letting the joy of being human, the joy of being children and images of God, and the joy of friendship in the Lord shine forth to others in your whole being, in your love of life. This will really be God's glory shining forth in you, for his life in you shines forth in your warm love for all whom you meet.

Let this be your witness: I shall counteract the evil forces which are against life, such as the evil of abortion, not primarily by severe penances inflicted upon myself, but above all by my love of life, living it in all its fullness, filled with the joy of being a child of God, of being an apostle of this joy by the very joy which radiates forth from my heart, with all its light and warmth and vitality, the joy which reaches its fullness only in friendship in the Lord, for our joy in the wonders God has done for us is complete only in sharing it with others.

TWELVE

LOVE'S REVERENCE: THE SPIRIT OF CELIBACY

There is no true love without reverence. And reverence is always tender. One who is precious, appreciated, reverenced is never treated roughly. He is cherished, nourished, tended. Reverently, tenderly, love calls forth all that is best in the loved one. He is invited to unfold and blossom, to give fragrance, to shine with light and beauty, to sing with joyous melody, to radiate life and warmth and light, to captivate with his charm and strength and joy those who love him.

My loving reverence for you results from my loving appreciation of your true value. You are precious and lovable beyond all imagining, sheerly because you are a person created by God.

To say that you are a person is to say that you are made for love. As a person, you cannot live without loving. Only in love does your beauty unfold. Only in loving do you become truly yourself. Only in love are you fully alive. Only when you are fully alive do you glorify God and shine with his radiance.

My love for you, my appreciation of your value, finds its joy in promoting this value, calling it forth by inviting your love, inspiring your love by my love for you. You are most fully precious and lovable only when you love. My love for you and my joy in you increase when you respond to my love, loving in return, becoming more lovable, and enriching me by your love. And the richer I am, the more precious I am to your love for me. And the richer we are together.

To love you is to desire that you be as lovable as possible, and that I be as loving as possible. To want you to be as lovable as possible is to want you to be your true self, your best self. But since you were made for love, you are most fully yourself only when you are fully loving.

To be fully loving, and therefore fully lovable, you must love not just me but all those whom you can love and ought to love. In loving all whom you love, you desire that each one of these be as lovable as possible by being as loving as possible, each loving as many others as he or she can and ought to love.

Thus, to love you is to desire a whole network of lovers. Loving you in this way, I love with universal love. I reach out to embrace all whom I can love myself, and through you I embrace all those whom you love, and all those whom these in turn are loving. We are all knit together in love. True love loves everyone. Jesus Christ came to establish universal brotherhood.

My true love for you requires reverence not only for you but also for myself. If I am to enrich you to the maximum by my gift of self to you in love, I must become my truest self. To be as loving as possible toward you is to be all that I possibly can be for you. I can be the most for you only by becoming my best possible self.

That is why love for you requires profound reverence for myself, and the refusal to be less for you, even if you ask it, than I ought to be. Genuine love for you forbids me to degrade myself to indulge your ill-considered and ignoble desires. My love for you, if it is true, refuses to let me degrade myself before you. It will not let you drag me from my ideals and responsibilities. It will not permit you to hamper me in becoming the self God meant me to be. Refusing to be my true self is a refusal to be for you!

Therefore, if your love for me is mature, you want me to be free to be my best self. You refuse to mold me possessively to your own narrow selfishness. Rather, your love for me is overjoyed in seeing that I am beloved of God and faithful to him. It rejoices in seeing how I enrich others, too, by my love and friendship for them.

My love for you, desiring that you be as enriched as possible by this love, desires then not only that you be your true self but that, for you, I be my true self: my self as friend of God, as belonging to the Lord and in the service of his love, loving universally all whom he has given me to love.

When I am as loving as possible in loving you, I rejoice, too, that you are so lovable in loving all whom you can love. I am happy that you are happy in so many friends.

These things are true of all love, even the love of husband and wife. For a man's love for his wife does not prevent her from having many friends. He is all the happier the richer and happier she is in friendly relationships: in loving her children, her neighbors, her friends, all upon whom she can radiate her love. No true friendship is ever a completely closed circle closed in upon just two. Each friendship must be open to the larger human community.

The wife's love for her husband, in turn, is all the happier the more she sees how his love for his fellowmen radiates far and wide. The woman who loves me sends me out to love others and thus become my true self, the man of influence I ought to be. Not the influence of wealth and power and selfish manipulation of others, even under the pretext that I am doing this for love of my wife and family, but the influence of loving kindness, which cherishes and nourishes love and goodness in every person it meets.

If his love for me were possessive, the person who loves me would be stifling my power to love; he would be preventing me from the fullness of love. This is true of possessive friends and possessive mothers as well as of possessive wives or possessive husbands. But because my friend's love is so concerned that I be fully myself, loving as I ought, he freely lets me go forth to love; he sends me forth to radiate goodness.

For he wants me to return to him with a multitude of others who love me and enrich me by their love. In these he too can rejoice because of the happiness and fullness of life I find in loving them. His love for me desires that I become rich in giving to others and promoting their happiness, and in being true to myself by loving fully, fulfilling my God-given mission to love.

But if two friends are totally closed in upon themselves, they live in a selfishness-for-two which only compounds the selfishness of two individuals. Thus, for example, husband and wife in their love for each other must be open to the whole community in which they live. As unselfish love of husband and wife matures, it becomes ever more open to others, beginning first of all with their children, and spreading wider and wider as each member of the family encircles more and more persons in love and friendship. The marriage friendship, like every true friendship, is open to the larger community and fully integrated into it through loving exchange.

Yet in conjugal love there are psychological factors which can hinder the growth of the all-embracing love and hamper it in reaching out far and wide. Husband and wife are so captivated with each other that ever so much of their energy goes into pleasing each other and into caring for each other. It is only right that it should be so. But they are not as free to love universally as is the truly loving celibate, the celibate who is consecrated to the Lord as a mediator of his love. St. Paul speaks of this with remarkable psychological insight when he says that the unmarried man, or the virgin, is anxious about the affairs of the Lord, how to be holy in body and spirit, but the married man, or the married woman, is anxious about worldly affairs, how to please his wife, or her husband, and is divided (1 Cor 7:32–35).

When he says that the celibate is anxious to be "holy in body and spirit" (1 Cor 7:34), Paul makes it clear that he is speaking of a consecration to the Lord. The word "holy" is a cultic one, indicating consecrated service of the Lord, a total belonging for the advance of his affairs. His affairs are those of his kingdom. His kingdom is his reign in covenant love; his kingdom is the communion of men with God their Father and with all their brothers in Christ, in the universal love poured out into our hearts by the Holy Spirit who is given to us (Rom 5:5).

If it is easier for the celibate to attain to universal love because all of his or her energies are consecrated to the reign of love, this does not mean that the married cannot attain to it. They are under the same Christian obligation as the celibate to strive for universal love, for they, too, are commanded to love the Lord their God with all their heart and soul and strength, and neighbor as self. The sign value of celibacy consists precisely in this: As consecration to the fullness of love, it is a challenge to all mankind, including the married, to be knit together in universal love. Christians love one another because God has put his own love into their hearts. Therefore, married love can be as open to fellowmen as celibate love, for both one and the other are a participation in Christ's own love. Who has not had experience of this, who has not known, for example, a Christian woman, wife and mother, whose heart has gone out to everyone who needs help and comfort and encouragement and is ever ready with time and energy to aid those who need her?

LOVE'S DISTANCE: THE SPIRIT OF CELIBACY

Love can attain its greatest fullness and richness only when there is a certain distance between the friends. If I hold the one I love too possessively, I hamper his growth. I do not let him grow in other loving relationships. I impoverish him and even deprive him of his freedom to love me.

I must give my friend distance so that he may be truly himself even in loving me, so that he may come to me freely, in love, and not by my demand. If I am forever forcing myself upon him and demanding his love, he has lost his freedom to give his love. For love cannot be forced, it can only be given. If he has no freedom to give his love on his own initiative rather than on my demand, he cannot be truly himself, his fully loving self.

This is true also in my relationship with God. Prayer is never demanding. In humility, I await the goodness of God's love. I wait in eager desire and expectancy, yes, but never saying how or when the signs of God's love are to be given.

I must give my friend distance, moreover, not only so that he can be fully free in loving me, but so that he can be fully himself in loving others, developing these other friendships and, above all, his friendship with God.

Authentic love includes reverence for the other not simply as person, one capable of establishing loving relationships, but as the person God wants him to be. God intends that he should live in loving relationship with him. Only in this relationship with God can he be fully a person.

This means that I have to give my friend distance so that he has freedom to be with God. My love does not rightly reverence him if I hold him so exclusively for myself that I hinder his approach to God.

That is why St. Paul, in the same breath in which he speaks of the holiness of conjugal intercourse, speaks also of going beyond this intercourse for the sake of direct communion with God. "The wife cannot claim her body as her own; it is her husband's. Equally, the husband cannot claim his body as his own; it is his wife's. Do not deny yourselves to one another, unless perhaps by mutual consent for a time, to devote yourselves to prayer" (1 Cor 7:5).

Here we are very close to the deepest reason for Christian celibacy. In their mutual reverence for each other as persons created for communion with God, husband and wife give each other enough distance so that each can be his or her true self in communion with God. They live the *spirit of celibacy* in seeking to belong first of all to the Lord and letting each other belong to him. The spirit of celibacy is a reverence for self, and for others, as made for communion with God. It lets the other have his distance so he can be with God, and it takes distance from others and from all things for the sake of direct communion with the Lord.

When friends are narrowly possessive of one another, they deprive one another of this freedom to love God and to become their truest self in communion with him. When in love they are too closed in upon themselves, their love becomes an obstacle between them and God, whereas it was really meant by God to be a way to him.

Fallen mankind easily enough falls into this selfish exclusiveness in love, using one another for one's own advantage rather than reverencing one another as being created for openness to God and fellowmen in universal love.

That is why Christian celibacy must exist alongside Christian marriage. Christian celibacy is a striking witness to the direct communion with God which is at the deepest heart of all Christian existence, even Christian marriage. All authentic love is celibate in this sense, that in reverence for the other it lets him have his distance, so that he has freedom to find his truest self in communion with God.

In becoming this, he can be all the more for me, his friend, when he turns back to me in love. His love for me is not impoverished by his love for God, it is infinitely enriched.

All reverence for those I love partakes of the spirit of celibacy. All standing aside, giving my friend his distance so that he can be his true self without interference from selfishness and possessiveness on my part, is a kind of celibacy. It is an abstention from my own pleasure in possessing my loved one so that he can be his true self, the self God meant him to be.

This is the spirit in which parents abstain from being too possessive of their growing sons and daughters and give them the freedom to become their own true selves. This is the spirit in which consecrated celibates love one another, their friends, and all whom God has given them to love. This is the spirit in which any true friend loves his friend.

The spirit of celibacy is letting my friend have his freedom to love God, to love me, to love his friends, to love all who need his love. It is letting him belong to the Lord and to be at the service of his mission of love.

THE REALITY OF CELIBACY

The spirit of celibacy finds its fullest concrete expression in the actual reality of consecrated celibacy, whose deepest purpose is to belong totally to the Lord alone and to be engaged exclusively with his affairs. And his affairs, we said, are the advance of his kingdom: the communion of all men with God their Father and with all their brothers in Christ, in the universal love poured out into our hearts by the Holy Spirit who is given to us.

One can be engaged exclusively with the Lord's affairs only by belonging totally to the Lord. Consecration to his work is necessarily rooted in consecration to his Person. Thus, in its deepest essence, consecrated celibacy is consecration to the Lord himself in a kind of spiritual marriage in which one is completely open to him for the fullness of communion with him. Celibacy is thus rooted in prayer and cannot survive without prayer.

Celibacy is not only a direct relationship with God; it is a relationship also with everyone whom we love in the Lord. The spirit of celibacy must govern all Christian relationships, whether with God or with fellowmen, with husband or wife, with parents or children, with friends or with strangers.

PRIESTLY AND RELIGIOUS CELIBACY

So, too, the celibacy of a priest or of a religious is not mere abstention from sexual union. More fundamentally, it is a spirit of reverence for the Lord and for everyone else as belonging to the Lord. It is reverence for what the Lord is doing in self and in others by the working of his Holy Spirit.

Celibacy as an apostolic quality is not mere freedom from family cares so as to be more available in the apostolate. In its aspects as relationship with others, the priest's celibacy, and that of the religious, is a deep reverence for all those in his charge. What he wants above all else for them is that they be the Lord's! He is not possessive of them. He does not want them for his own glory, like the preacher who is trying to make a name for himself by his preaching or who wants a following only to reassure himself that he is a success, or an important person.

Like John the Baptist, he fades away before the Lord. "He who has the bride is the Bridegroom. . . . He must increase, I must decrease" (Jn 3:29, 30). Like Paul, he presents his Church (and each of the persons in his charge who are that Church) as a chaste virgin to the Lord.

Certainly, such an apostolic attitude presupposes that he himself is the Lord's. "I am racing to grasp the prize, if possible, since I have been grasped by Christ Jesus. . . . My entire attention is on the finish line as I run toward the prize to which God calls me—life on high in Christ Jesus" (Phil 3:12–14).

Celibacy, then, is far more than purity in the sense of bodily abstention from sex. It is the purity of heart which desires only the Lord, for self and for others. It is purity from all desire and intent to manipulate others for one's own advantage. It is freedom from all use of others for one's own purposes. The celibate is free of the impurity of delighting in adulation and flattery or craving attention as though he were the Lord! Celibacy is reverence for what is most precious in all persons: their direct communion with the Lord.

Therefore, celibacy can rejoice in intimate friendships with those who are the Lord's. It overflows with joy at seeing the wonders which the Lord is working in the loved ones. It experiences what John the Evangelist meant when he says that he proclaims the Gospel about the Word so that his own joy will be full in bringing others into the communion which he himself enjoys with the Father and with his Son Jesus Christ (1 Jn 1:3–4). Celibacy experiences the joy of John the Baptist in bringing everyone to the Lord. "He who has the bride is the Bridegroom; the friend of the Bridegroom, who stands and hears him, rejoices greatly at the Bridegroom's voice. Therefore this joy of mine is now full" (Jn 3:29). Those who respond to the voice of the Bridegroom with faith in his word are espoused as a chaste virgin to the Word himself. The celibate's most profound joys come in seeing how his friends love the Lord!

EPILOGUE

"KNIT TOGETHER IN LOVE"

The Stoic philosophers spoke of a mysterious sort of fluid called *pneuma*, or spirit, which fills the universe, holding all things together, keeping them from disintegrating and dispersing.

What the Stoics attributed to this *pneuma*, the author of the Book of Wisdom attributes to God's own Spirit. Through his Spirit, God is everywhere present and powerful: "The Spirit of the Lord fills the world, and holds all things together" (Ws 1:7).

A little later in his book, this author says something similar about wisdom. Wisdom, he says, "pervades all spirits, though they be intelligent, pure and very subtle. For wisdom is mobile beyond all motion, and she penetrates and pervades all things by reason of her purity" (Ws 7:23-24). Thus, wisdom seems to be identical with the Spirit of the Lord "which holds all things together" (Ws 1:7).

Paul, in a passage influenced by all the wisdom writings of the Old Testament, applies to Christ what was said of wisdom. In Christ, he says, "all things hold together" (Col 1:17). In Proverbs, wisdom was called "the first-born" begotten by God before anything was made (Prv 8:22). Paul calls Christ "the first-born of all creatures," in whom "everything in heaven and on earth was created," and "in him all things hold together" (Col 1:15–17).

If we read these words without reference to the rest of the letter to the Colossians, and without reference to Ephesians which further expands the thought of Colossians, we might think that Christ holds all things together only by his creating and sustaining power. But Paul sees Christ as far more than Creator upholding all things by his power, or even by his love, though it is his love which is expressed in the act of creation and in the maintenance of that creation. Paul is thinking of Christ's love holding all things together in a more marvelous way than as a power giving them existence.

The Stoics were speaking of the physical elements of the universe being held together by the *pneuma*. The author of the Book of Wisdom was speaking not only of physical elements but also of the persons and hearts of men: "God is witness of man's inmost feelings and a true observer of his heart and a hearer of his tongue; because the Spirit of the Lord has filled the world, and that which holds all things together knows what is said" (Ws 1:7). In other words, God knows our hearts and our words because he pervades and upholds all things by his presence and power.

But Paul takes the matter to a more sublime level when he says that Christ's own divine love, poured out into the hearts of men in the giving of the Holy Spirit, is the bond holding all things together and bringing everything into unity in his Holy Spirit. "Christ's love holds me, impels me," says Paul (2 Cor 5:14). Paul is using the same Greek verb used in Wisdom in saying that the Spirit of the Lord "holds all things together" (Ws 1:7). By thus alluding to the Book of Wisdom, Paul is giving a more profound insight into how Christ and his Spirit fill the universe and hold all things together. The risen Lord, whose body is totally penetrated, glorified, transformed by the Holy Spirit, fills the whole universe and holds it together. The Lord unites the universe not simply by his Holy Spirit filling all things but by God's own love formed in the hearts of men by the Holy Spirit who fills these hearts and dwells in them, God's own love operative in these hearts and knitting them together in love.

Paul speaks of God's own love operative in Paul's own heart: "Christ's love holds me. presses, urges me" (2 Cor 5:14). Christ's love *possesses* me, impelling me to carry on the ministry of reconciliation of all mankind in that same love (2 Cor 5:13–15). Christ's love in men's hearts impels them to unity and reconciliation (2 Cor 5:18–19). Thus, it is Christ's love operative in us which unites the universe and holds it together.

All things hold together in that love, not simply that love as Holy Spirit and creative power, but that love as responded to by our love, our love responding in that love. For God's own love is poured out into our hearts by the Holy Spirit who is given to us from the heart of Christ (Rom 5:5). In that love, given to us by the Holy Spirit, we respond to Jesus and the Father (Rom 8:15). And in that love, Christ's own love in us, we respond to one another, all God's children. Thus, we are knit together in love in such a way that in that love all things hold together. But this love is ever being caused and sustained in us by the very Person of the Holy Spirit dwelling in us, for love in the Lord is a participation in the Holy Spirit.

THE FULLNESS OF CHRIST

Paul tells us all of this by using another term borrowed from the philosophy of the Stoics: the *pleroma*, the fullness. "The God of glory," says Paul, "raised Jesus from the dead and seated him at his right hand in heaven. . . . He has put all things under his feet and has made him head of the Church, which is his body, the fullness of him who fills *all in all*" (Eph 1:20–23).

In Sirach, the universe was called the fullness of God, and God was said to be "all in all" because he fills all things by his presence through his creative and unifying power (Sir 43:28). In Ephesians, the Church is called "the fullness of Jesus who fills *all in all*" (Eph 1:23) because he fills the Church with his Holy Spirit, the life-giving power of his resurrection, and thus makes the Church his body. And through the Church, he fills the universe, which he restores and reconciles to God so that in a new way "God is all in all" (1 Cor 15:28), in a more marvelous way than Sirach ever dreamed of.

Wherever the Church is coming into being because men are being filled with the Spirit of the risen Jesus, the personal risen body of the Lord Jesus is already present, filling believers with his Holy Spirit, incorporating them into this body, until his body the Church fills the universe. Thus, in the body of Christ, his risen body expanded into his body the Church, God's creatures are filled with his own divine life in the Holy Spirit. The Church is the fullness of Christ, for she is filled with Christ as Christ himself is filled with God. "For in Christ," says Paul, "the fullness of divinity resides in bodily form, and in him you share in this fullness" (Col 2:9).

The Church is the fullness of the risen Lord, not in the sense that she adds anything to him, but in the sense that he fills her with divine life in the Holy Spirit, and through her works to sanctify all mankind with this divine life. The Church is Christ's body because all the spiritual power of the risen body of Christ is possessed by her. She is his fullness because she has the fullness of Christ's Spirit and life and power.

But in another sense, as through her sanctifying power more and more of mankind is incorporated into the body of Christ, she is growing up to the fullness, "to the mature measure of the fullness of Christ, growing up in every way into him who is the head, into Christ, from whom the whole body, joined and knit together, makes bodily growth and upbuilds itself in love" (Eph 4:13–16).

And in this body of Christ, the Church, we are "filled unto all the fullness of God" (Eph 3:19) because we are filled with the knowledge or experience of Christ's love which surpasses all knowledge (3:19). That is, the fullness of God's own life given to us in Christ is the experience of God's own love, that love communicated in Christ to the length and breadth and height and depth of the universe (3:18), filling the hearts of men so that they are "knit together in love" (Col 2:2). In the very love uniting men, God's own love is experienced, and in this love all things hold together. God dwells in this love as in a temple, for in this love he is possessed and adored and embraced. "Christ himself is the cornerstone, in whom the whole structure is joined together and grows into a holy temple in the Lord; in whom you also are built into it for a dwelling place of God in the Spirit" (Eph 2:20).

All things hold together in a living communion with God. We know God even as we are known (Gal 4:9). To know God, in scriptural language, means to experience him in love. It means to experience his love for us in our love responding to his. "I know my sheep and my sheep know me in the same way that the Father knows me and I know the Father" (Jn 10:15). The Christian communion is a participation in the communion of knowledge and love which is the very life of the three divine Persons.

Thus, all things hold together in God's love for us given to us in the Spirit in Christ and our love in response. The universe holds together in love only when mankind receives God's gift of love in the Holy Spirit and, in this love, builds up the body of Christ in love. It does not happen as if by magic, it comes about only by our cooperation. Therefore Paul, after telling us that the Church is the fullness of Christ who fills all in all, insists that we must grow up to this fullness: "Make every effort to preserve the unity which has the Spirit as its origin and peace as its binding force. There is but one body and one Spirit, just as there is but one hope given all of you by your call. There is one Lord, one faith, one baptism: one God and Father of all, who is over all, and works through all, and is in all" (Eph 4:3–6).

Through this love by which he holds all things together, Jesus rules the universe. His kingdom is effectively established to the extent that all things hold together in the love which he himself forms in our hearts by his Holy Spirit, fruit of his paschal sacrifice. For surrendering his human spirit to the Father in his death on the cross, he receives the Holy Spirit, whom he pours out into our hearts, filling these hearts with love of God and one another.

This glorious fullness of the Holy Spirit knitting us together in love is possible only through our dying to self. Jesus, the suffering servant, came to his exaltation as Lord only through his obedient death on the cross. Only through his sacrificial death in humble obedience did he receive this Spirit whom he poured out upon us.

Therefore, Paul presents the suffering Servant (Phil 2:5–11) as the model of the humble Christian service without which we cannot be knit together in love (Phil 2:1–4). The basic way of dying with Christ, that we might receive the fullness of his Holy Spirit uniting us in love, is death to the selfishness which sets us against one another, killing this selfishness in the love expressed in humble mutual service and presence to one another, the love communicated to us in the eucharistic celebration.

> So if there is any encouragement in Christ, any incentive of love, any participation in the Spirit, any affection and sympathy, complete my joy by being of the same mind, having the same love, being of full accord and of one mind. Do nothing from selfishness or conceit, but in humility count others better than yourselves. Let each of you look not to his own interests, but also to the interests of others. Have this mind in you, which you have in Christ Jesus, who, though he was in the form of God, did not count equality with God a thing to be grasped, but emptied himself, taking the form of a servant . . . (Phil 1:1ff.)

AFTERWORD

BY SR. MIRIAM JAMES HEIDLAND, SOLT

> Friends in the Lord always turn one another toward the Lord. They are not forever gazing at each other, but together they look to the Lord and to their brothers and sisters in the Lord.
>
> —Paul Hinnebusch, OP,
> *Friendship in the Lord* (101)

When I first read this book many years ago, it forever changed my view of friendship and how to honor and reverence the Lord, myself, and others. As I have pondered the many friendships in my own life over the years, I have seen both joy and sorrow, darkness and light. In rereading this work by Fr. Paul Hinnebusch, I was filled again with the desire to give to the Lord every relationship in my life and receive each one of them again through his heart.

As you read this book, you may have noticed your own heart swelling with the desire to find a way to belong with another person, to have a friend who understands you, who is kind and who calls you to excellence. A friend with whom you can laugh, be yourself, share the deep places of your heart, and be at rest. A friend who will not leave you or forsake you, a friend who is not jealous or envious, a friendship that is free, life-giving, and grace-filled. A friendship based on goodness, virtue, and holiness. Such a desire echoes with our ache for heaven.

But how can we practically live this beautiful vision of friendship this side of eternity? Although we will always struggle with our own fallenness, I think three things are key to finding and living within relationships that lead us to holiness.

First: We belong to God above all. Fr. Hinnebusch reminds us that our whole being desires to turn to the Lord and to receive from him our identity and ultimate love. As he states throughout the book, when we turn to anyone else to give us our identity and ultimate love, we make an idol out of the person or the thing to which we turn. Only God can give those realities, confirm them, and sustain them. We belong to him, first and foremost.

We must ask the Lord daily to order and purify our loves. When we find our eyes turning away from the primacy of the Lord, we must be very honest about those movements of our heart and ask his help to return to him. As Song of Songs 2:4 reads in Latin, "*Ordinavit in me caritatem*"—You have set love in order in me. The more we allow the Lord to order our loves, the more we can truly love others and be loved by them in return.

Second: We need ongoing personal healing. We must know ourselves in the Lord. Where in your life has love been broken and lost? Where do you turn when you feel threatened, afraid, or lonely? What are the patterns of sin and disorder in your life? What "fig leaves" are most comfortable to you when you experience shame and fear? What is the landscape of your life story?

Although most of us would rather not engage these tender places and sorrowful mysteries of our lives, we must do so. We are invited to encounter these places with the Lord, not by ourselves. The unhealed wounds and dark corners of our lives are often the gateways and foundation of disintegration and disorder within us. We have all had the experience of running away from pain only to find ourselves in a much worse situation. What seems like a way out only leads to deeper loneliness and sorrow.

The good news is that Jesus offers us a way through the brokenness in which we find ourselves. His own Passion, Death, and Resurrection—the Paschal Mystery—become a beautiful path for us to new life. He is our only way through the darkness and death of sin—through him, with him, and in him, we find life and freedom.

The lifelong task of following him is a journey of healing in which he makes us more and more capable of receiving and giving love. In him, we come to see that we are lovable even in the most painful places. Our task is to turn away from living in lies and sin and darkness and turn toward Jesus, who is the Way, the Truth and the Life (see John 14:6). More and more, little by little, this path of healing allows us to love as Jesus loves.

Third: We must receive others as gift. When we receive a gift, our hands and our hearts are open and receptive. We do not turn to grasping, controlling, dominating, or possessing. We can only enjoy the beauty of something when we receive it from God and freely return it back to him, for in truth, as all the spiritual masters write, everything truly good is just a small, minute reflection of God himself. When we try to possess and grasp and make things happen for ourselves, we ruin and mar the gift. When we ask for the grace to receive everything and everyone in our lives as a gift from God, our hearts and hands remain open, even in the midst of painful purifications.

Love and friendship are great and wonderful gifts from God. Our friendship with him, with ourselves, and with others make life beautiful and meaningful. These relationships augment our joy and console us in loss. We are made for this type of living—we are made for this type of love. For every true friendship in the Lord reveals a foretaste of heaven, wherein communion, belonging, joy, freedom, wonder, glory, light, and love unite in God and marvelously grow forever, without end.

NOTES

3. THE FRIENDSHIP OF CATHERINE AND RAYMOND

1. *Saint Catherine of Siena as Seen in Her Letters*, ed. and trans. Vida D. Scudder (J. M. Dent & Sons, 1927), 326.

2. *Saint Catherine of Siena*, 327.

3. *Saint Catherine of Siena*, 326.

4. Rudolf Bultmann, *Glauben und Verstehen I* (Tübingen, 1964), 240.

5. St. Thomas Aquinas, *Summa Theologiae*, III, q. 26.

6. *Saint Catherine of Siena*, 331.

7. *Saint Catherine of Siena*, 326.

8. *Saint Catherine of Siena*, 328.

9. St. Francis de Sales, *Letters to Persons in Religion*, trans. Henry B. Mackey (Newman, 1943), 93–94.

10. St. Francis de Sales, *Letters*, 159.

11. St. Francis de Sales, *Letters*, 94.

12. St. Francis de Sales, *Letters*, 159.

13. Gerald Vann, *To Heaven With Diana* (Pantheon, 1960), 84. All of Jordan's letters are available in this volume.

14. St. Francis de Sales to St. Jane Frances de Chantal, quoted by A. Ple, "Celibacy and the Emotional Life," *Clergy Review* 55 (1970), 42.

5. LOVING APPRECIATION IN ADULT FRIENDSHIPS

1. St. Teresa of Avila strongly recommends sharing in spiritual conversation, especially to those who are beginners in the serious life of prayer. See her *Life*, in *The Complete Works of St.*

Teresa of Jesus, trans. and ed. E. Allison Peers (Sheed & Ward, 1944), 46ff.

2. The word *intimacy* is likely to have sexual connotations for some people, and, therefore, we point out that whenever in this book we speak of the intimacy of human friendship, we use the word *intimacy* in the sense described earlier. Intimacy, we said, means being fully at home with someone. Home is where I am fully known and loved and received just as I am. Only in trusted love do I have intimacy.

9. FRIENDSHIP IN THE SPIRIT

1. *The Dialogue of St. Catherine of Siena* (Newman, 1950), 110ff. We present Catherine's words slightly paraphrased, to make her thought stand out more clearly for the modern reader.

2. Abraham Maslow, chap. 3 in *Toward a Psychology of Being* (Van Nostrand, 1968).

PAUL HINNEBUSCH, OP (1917–2002), was a renowned author, scholar, and spiritual guide whose writings continue to inspire readers in the pursuit of prayer, friendship, religious life, and knowledge of scripture. He authored more than one hundred articles and at least eighteen books, including *Friendship in the Lord*, *Community in the Lord*, and *Prayer, the Search for Authenticity*. A member of the Dominican Order—like six of his nine siblings—he dedicated his life to educating and guiding others in the faith.

Ordained in 1944, Hinnebusch earned degrees from the Aquinas Institute of Theology and Duquesne University before embarking on a distinguished teaching career. Over nearly two decades, he lectured at a number of colleges, including the University of Notre Dame, St. Mary's Dominican College, the University of Dallas, and St. Louis University. In recognition of his contributions to the study of scripture and the theology of the spiritual life, the Dominican Order awarded him a master of sacred theology degree in 1994.

Hinnebusch's deep commitment to spiritual formation extended beyond the classroom. He mentored novices of the Dominican sisters in Louisiana and served as a spiritual director for the Missionaries of Charity in Texas.

FR. JOHN BURNS is a priest of the Archdiocese of Milwaukee and the founder of Friends of the Bridegroom, an apostolate dedicated to renewing the Church through the healing, restoration, and expansion of women's religious life in America. He is the author of the bestselling books *Lift Up Your Heart: A 10-Day Personal Retreat with St. Francis de Sales*, *Adore: A Guided Advent Journal for Prayer and Meditation*, and *Return: A Guided Lent Journal for Prayer and Meditation*.

SR. MIRIAM JAMES HEIDLAND, SOLT, is a popular Catholic speaker, a cohost of the *Abiding Together* podcast, and the author of the bestselling books *Loved as I Am*, *Restore: A Guided Lent Journal for Prayer and Meditation*, and *Behold: A Guided Advent Journal for Prayer and Meditation*.

Heidland is also affiliated with the Friends of the Bridegroom community and the John Paul II Healing Center. She leads healing retreats for priests and religious sisters across America.